Psychopathology

Psychopathology is a concise introduction to the major classes of adult mental illness. Beginning with an historical overview, the authors consider how mental abnormality can be defined, reviewing the main classification systems and the issues raised in classification and diagnosis. Schizophrenia, mood disorders, anxiety and eating disorders are explored with a description of the main features of illness, and the signs, symptoms and effects on behaviour for the patient, as well as the impact on relatives and friends. These issues are brought to life in a series of case studies which draw on the considerable clinical experience of both authors, and provide students with the opportunity to test their understanding.

Psychopathology is tailor-made for the student new to higher-level study, providing the factual knowledge needed to understand the key features of the major mental illnesses. With helpful textbook features provided to assist in examination and learning techniques, it should interest all introductory psychology students, as well as those training for the caring services, whether nurses, social workers, police officers or special needs teachers.

John D. Stirling is Senior Lecturer in Psychology at Manchester Metropolitan University. **Jonathan S.E. Hellewell** is a Consultant Community Psychiatrist at Trafford General Hospital in Manchester.

Routledge Modular Psychology

Series editors: Cara Flanagan is a Reviser for AS and A2 level Psychology and an experienced teacher and examiner. Philip Banyard is Associate Senior Lecturer in Psychology at Nottingham Trent University and a Chief Examiner for AS and A2 level Psychology.

The *Routledge Modular Psychology* series is a completely new approach to introductory-level psychology, tailor-made to the new modular style of teaching. Each short book covers a topic in more detail than any large textbook can, allowing teacher and student to select material exactly to suit any particular course or project.

The books have been written especially for those students new to higher-level study, whether at school, college or university. They include specially designed features to help with technique, such as a model essay at an average level with an examiner's comments to show how extra marks can be gained. The authors are all examiners and teachers at the introductory level.

The *Routledge Modular Psychology* texts are all user-friendly and accessible and use the following features:

- practice essays with specialist commentary to show how to achieve a higher grade
- chapter summaries to assist with revision
- progress and review exercises
- glossary of key terms
- summaries of key research
- further reading to stimulate ongoing study and research
- cross-referencing to other books in the series

For more details on our AS, A2 and *Routledge Modular Psychology* publications visit our website at www.a-levelpsychology.co.uk

Also available in this series (titles listed by syllabus section):

Psychopathology

*John D. Stirling and
Jonathan S.E. Hellewell*

Routledge
Taylor & Francis Group

LONDON AND NEW YORK

First published 1999
by Routledge
11 New Fetter Lane, London EC4P 4EE

Simultaneously published in the USA and Canada
by Routledge
29 West 35th Street, New York, NY 10001

Reprinted 2005 by Routledge
27 Church Road, Hove, East Sussex, BN3 2FA
270 Madison Avenue, New York NY 10016

Routledge is an imprint of the Taylor & Francis Group

Typeset in Times by Routledge
Printed and bound in Great Britain by TJ International Ltd, Padstow, Cornwall

British Library Cataloguing in Publication Data
A catalogue record for this book is available from the British Library

Library of Congress Cataloguing in Publication Data
Psychopathology / John D. Stirling and Jonathan S.E. Hellewell.
(Routledge modular psychology)
Includes bibliographical references and index.
1. Psychology, Pathological. I. Hellewell, Jonathon S.E.
II. Title. III. Series
RC454.S775   1999   98-33124
616.89-dc21   CIP

ISBN 0–415–19270–6 (hbk)
ISBN 0–415–19271–4 (pbk)

Contents

List of tables

Acknowledgements

The series editors and Routledge acknowledge the expert help of Paul Humphreys, Examiner and Reviser for A-Level Psychology, in compiling the Study Aids section of each book in this series.

We also acknowledge the Associated Examining Board (AEB) for permission to use their examination material. The AEB do not accept responsibility for the answers or examiner comment in the Study Aids section of this book or in any book in the series.

All case studies in *Psychopathology* are fictitious and do not relate specifically to any person in particular.

1

A framework for scientific psychopathology

Introduction

Psychopathology is the scientific study of abnormal behaviour. As such it differs from both **clinical psychology** and **psychiatry** which respectively focus on behavioural and medical management of mental disorder. However, it draws heavily on research material from both disciplines, as well as dipping into the literature from psychology, neurology and the medical sciences in general. It is a bridging discipline, which covers topics as diverse as stress management, brain biochemistry and molecular genetics.

Historical background

Despite rumours to the contrary, there is nothing new about mental illness. Descriptions of abnormal behaviour can be found amongst the historical records of the first civilizations and it is certain that the early Egyptians, Chinese, Greeks and Incas were familiar with the features of disturbed behaviour that we may, today, identify as mental illness. Sadly, it also seems that for much of recorded history such people have found themselves marginalised, shunned or ridiculed, with their symptoms variously attributed to the processes of demonic possession, divine punishment, planetary influence or witchcraft.

More than 2,000 years ago, the Greek philosophers Hippocrates and Plato argued that mental illnesses had more commonplace causes: physiological dysfunction in the case of Hippocrates and psychological conflict in the case of Plato. However, at the time, their ideas generally fell on deaf ears. Indeed, records for the next 1,500 years are very sketchy, although we know that this period of European history (known as the Dark and Middle Ages) was marked by a decline in rational scientific thinking and a return to religious superstition. The perilous position of mentally ill individuals was illustrated in 1484, when the Pope issued a decree reminding his emissaries that sudden loss of reason, amongst other signs, should be regarded as one of the features of demonic possession, for which the appropriate action was burning at the stake!

Mental derangement or mental illness?

The idea that mentally deranged people might actually be ill first began to reappear at the time of major population shifts from rural to urban dwelling. As cities got larger, municipal authorities gave themselves powers to incarcerate people who appeared to be mentally unwell. Initially, specific provision for the mentally unwell was restricted to a handful of institutions. For example, the Priory of Saint Mary of Bethlehem, founded in 1243, developed a facility for housing a small number of people with mental illness, which somewhat later was handed over to the City of London as an institution specifically for this purpose. Its name became corrupted and as **Bedlam** it developed a degree of notoriety as a sort of tourist attraction, which people could visit to observe the behaviour of the inmates, both male and female. (Astonishingly, this practice continued well into the 1800s.)

Moral treatment

The French Revolution in the late 1700s brought about a marked change in the methods of dealing with mentally ill people. The French physician Philippe Pinel was shocked to see the conditions under which the inmates of asylums were expected to live and, in the spirit of revolution, called for their unchaining. Pinel, with his enlightened approach, known as **moral treatment**, attracted the attention of other like-minded individuals and gradually a change in attitude towards how best to manage mentally ill people spread through western Europe. For example, William Tuke, a Quaker, persuaded others from his religious group to fund the building of a mental hospital, The York Retreat, which was founded in 1796. Here, patients received care and treatments similar to those advocated by Pinel.

Ironically, the success of moral treatment also contributed to its downfall in the latter stages of the nineteenth century, as it became apparent that mental illness was much more common than had previously been thought. (Tuke's Retreat could accommodate only thirty patients.) As more people were recognised to be suffering from mental illness, major building programmes were instigated both in Europe and the United States, leading to the rapid growth in the number of state-run asylums for the mentally ill. Over a relatively short period in Victorian England, several hundred hospitals were built to accommodate many thousands of patients. The standards of care that prevailed in York could not be extended to these new hospitals and moral treatment fell out of favour.

The modern era: brain or mind?

Despite the inevitable deterioration in provision for mentally ill people, by the end of the century there was renewed interest in science and in the principle of **somatogenesis** which had first been described by Hippocrates 2,000 years earlier. It was against this background that the discipline of psychiatry began to emerge and the work of Kraepelin and Bleuler came to prominence. At that time, melancholia, mania and phrenitis, first described by Hippocrates, were identified as mental disorders, and this list was expanded to include paranoia, catatonia and hebephrenia, among many others.

Kraepelin's best known contribution to psychopathology was his proposal that mental illnesses can be divided into two broad syndromes: **dementia praecox** and **manic-depressive psychosis**. He reached this conclusion on the basis of detailed recording, over long periods of time, of the features (the **signs** and **symptoms**) of illness displayed by his patients. Although Bleuler disagreed with Kraepelin on matters of detail, he too adopted precise methods and his fascination with the nature and causes of psychiatric symptoms was a hallmark of his work. Between them, Kraepelin and Bleuler shaped the direction that psychiatry has subsequently taken and their contributions are still much in evidence today.

Kraepelin and Bleuler were convinced that mental illnesses had physical origins (the somatogenic approach). However, others believed that there were psychological (**psychogenic**) explanations of mental illness. These ideas had originally been discussed by Plato and they began to receive increasing attention once again. Mesmer (1734–1815) is often credited with initiating the renewed interest in psychogenesis, having 'invented' a form of hypnosis that came to be known as 'mesmerism'. In the late nineteenth century there was an explosion of interest in the role of psychological mechanisms in illness. Charcot, a prominent neurologist, demonstrated that symptoms characteristic of nerve damage could arise for psychological reasons and could be influenced by hypnotic suggestion. His colleague Breuer began using hypnosis as a treatment and it became apparent to him that, if he talked with his clients about their symptoms while they were under hypnosis, this often resulted in greater relief from symptoms. Breuer's technique became known as **catharsis** and was for a time adopted by another Viennese neurologist, Freud, who saw it as a potentially powerful means of exploring the **unconscious mind**.

In one or two sentences, summarise the main contributions to psychopathology of the following: Hippocrates, Kraepelin, Bleuler and Freud.

Progress exercise

The twentieth century and science

Our brief review has brought us to the beginning of the twentieth century. By this time most of the main ideas that have continued to dominate and shape the direction of modern psychopathology had already surfaced. During the past one hundred years, the pendulum has continued to swing between somatogenic and psychogenic explanations of disorder. Initially, the camps divided geographically, with the Europeans favouring somatogenesis, while practitioners in the United States preferred psychogenic explanations of mental illness. The divide has, to some extent, fallen along occupational lines, with medically trained psychiatrists resorting to somatogenic approaches and psychologists, not surprisingly, tending to rely upon psychogenic explanations.

One of the main strengths of psychopathology over the past century has been a willingness on the part of practitioners to rely on empirical evidence gathered through scientific research. This approach has, for example, led to the demise of unsupportable procedures such as **insulin coma therapy** (an early treatment for schizophrenia). On the other hand, it has established the advantages of equally controversial procedures such as **electro-convulsive therapy (ECT)**. Not all scientific discoveries have favoured somatogenic approaches. For example, the value of **biofeedback** training to help control anxiety and the adoption of a procedure known as **cognitive therapy** in the treatment of depression, both tend to support psychogenic arguments.

The stress-diathesis model

Gradually, research in psychopathology has made people aware that neither a strictly somatogenic or psychogenic approach can fully explain how mental illnesses arise. Indeed, evidence suggests that most occur as a result of a combination of factors, and a causal model known as the *stress-diathesis model* (Goldman 1992) has evolved to occupy this centre-ground. In simple terms, this model implies that mental illness is a reaction to life experiences in individuals who are vulnerable or predisposed in some way to that mental illness. One sort of predisposition may be genetic, but others may involve early brain damage or even early experience. The causative factors will inevitably vary, ranging from the effects of major and sudden life events such as bereavement or unemployment, to the minor but more enduring tensions of family life.

We consider the stress-diathesis model in the context of affective disorders in Chapter 6. For the time being, it is important to understand the difference between vulnerability (predisposition) and cause. Although research has shown that hereditary factors are important in manic-depressive illness, this does not mean that genes *cause* manic-depression; rather, that genetic factors *predispose* a person to developing this disorder. Meehl, the well-known psychopathologist, reinforced this point, commenting about another disorder in which hereditary factors seem important: he argued that while individuals do not inherit schizophrenia, they may inherit the predisposition to develop it (Meehl 1962).

One other point to clear up before the next section is our use of the term **aetiology**. In common with other people who work in the field of psychopathology, we use this term quite a lot. It may help if you think of it as another word for 'cause' or 'explanation'. Thus, when we discuss the *aetiology* of affective disorders (Chapter 6), we consider the various theories and approaches to unravelling the causes of these illnesses.

What is abnormal?

We now consider the difficult issue of distinguishing between normal and abnormal behaviour. It might help the reader to know at the outset that there are no simple solutions to this problem and although there are several ways of trying to establish abnormality, no single method is 'foolproof'. Often, a decision about whether or not an individual's behaviour is abnormal depends on a series of value judgements based on subjective impressions. (Remember that, unlike other branches of medicine, there are usually no tests or exploratory operations to guide the clinician in making a diagnosis.) In the following section we briefly summarise the strengths and weaknesses of each of the main approaches to this question.

Statistical infrequency

We know that behavioural measures, such as intelligence or short-term memory, tend to be normally distributed. That is to say that scores from a sample of people tend to fall into a 'bell-shaped curve'. Could we make use of this observation to define abnormality at the extremes of the distribution? In certain circumstances, for example at the bottom end of the IQ scale, this may work quite well – perhaps as a way of identifying children in need of special educational provision. But what about the other end of the scale? We imagine that anyone with an IQ of 150 (likely to occur in less than 0.5 per cent of the population) would be rather offended at the suggestion that they are abnormal! Clearly, this approach can at best offer limited assistance in our quest for criteria of abnormality.

Violation of norms

A second approach, introducing the idea of a social context, is to consider the extent to which behaviour deviates from the norm. It is, after all, rather unusual to wash one's hands several hundred times per day, as someone with *obsessive-compulsive disorder* might do. However, this criterion, when used in isolation, has serious limitations. For example, prostitution or criminal behaviour violate most people's norms, but surely do not in themselves constitute evidence of mental illness. Moreover, a social norm is, by definition, specific to a culture and it has been said, for example, that psychiatrists, being predominantly male, middle class and (in this country) white, may be ill-prepared to understand the behaviour and motivations of others from different social and cultural backgrounds.

Maladaptive behaviour

Maladaptive behaviours may be thought of as those that cause difficulties, or are counter-productive, for the individual or for others. The repetitive hand washing mentioned above could be regarded as maladaptive, particularly if it leads to sores or other skin damage. The self-starvation of a patient with severe *anorexia nervosa*, which sometimes leads to death, would be a second example. Yet would we consider that the self-destructive behaviour of a cigarette smoker constitutes evidence of mental illness? Clearly, as a way of identifying abnormality this approach is only partially successful and cannot be used on its own to guide psychiatric diagnosis.

Personal distress

Many patients with mental illness experience pronounced personal suffering. For example, patients with severe depression often describe feelings of anguish in addition to misery. Others express their distress in terms of physical complaints and may even visit their doctor believing that they are physically unwell. However, the subjective experience of the patient is not always a reliable indicator of illness, as some do not themselves acknowledge that they are ill. For example, patients with mania often say they feel ecstatic and euphoric, and in the early stages of schizophrenia the individual may be indifferent to or unaware of their deteriorating mental state.

Comment

Drawing the proverbial 'line in the sand' to distinguish between normal and abnormal behaviour is no simple matter and it is important to realise that neither the criteria for illness, nor the list of illnesses themselves, are *fixed*. Some critics have suggested that this state of uncertainty or ambiguity is likely to remain unless objective measures of illness are developed. However, the absence of these more objective measures, does not, in our view, undermine the continued search for them. Neither should it prevent attempts to refine the categories or diagnosis of mental illness.

Review exercise

What are the different approaches used in defining abnormality? List the advantages and shortcomings of each. Can you think of any other ways of identifying abnormal behaviour?

Summary

The debate about whether mental illnesses have somatogenic or psychogenic origins has dominated the history of psychopathology and can be traced back to the ideas of Hippocrates and Plato. Only recently have people begun to realise that mental disorders probably arise as a result of the combination of factors, rather than being due to single causes. Currently, interactionist models of causation, like the stress-diathesis model, find the widest acceptance in psychopathology. However, uncertainties remain about how best to define abnormal behaviour: at present, we tend to rely on a combination of criteria, each of limited value, and on the subjective assessments of clinicians.

Further reading

Davison, G.C. and Neale, J.M. (1998) *Abnormal Psychology*, 7th edn, New York: Wiley. The definitive general text of abnormal psychology. Although an American text, the approach is international. Superbly illustrated, very up-to-date, and comprehensive. Chapter 1 includes an excellent historical introduction.

2

Classification and paradigms of abnormal behaviour

Introduction

In psychopathology there are two main approaches to thinking about mental illness. One, known as the **idiopathic approach**, avoids classifying abnormal behaviour into diagnostic groupings. Instead, it analyses patients individually on their own merits. While this approach is favoured by some practitioners, it is nevertheless a minority perspective. The second is known as the **nomothetic approach** (so-called because it classifies and categorises disorders). As most people working in psychopathology feel that some sort of classification system is both helpful and necessary, this approach prevails. However, there are regular arguments about where boundaries between disorders should be drawn, and much time and energy has been spent in developing coherent systems of classification for common use throughout the world.

The ICD and DSM

Today, there are two major classification systems. The International Classification of Diseases, Injuries and Causes of Death (the ICD), developed by the World Health Organisation, covers mental and physical disorders. The Diagnostic and Statistical Manual (the DSM), which covers just mental disorders, has been developed by the American Psychiatric Association (APA). The ICD is now in its tenth version (ICD 10), and the DSM has been revised four times, most recently in 1994 (DSM IV). Although the DSM is used more extensively in the United States, while the ICD finds more favour in the United Kingdom and elsewhere in Europe, the reality is that, as far as psychopathology is concerned, the two systems have converged and now show considerable overlap.

Current versions of the ICD and DSM systems identify **operational diagnostic criteria** for each of the listed mental illnesses. This means that specific criteria must be met before a diagnosis can be made. Usually, there will be one or two core symptoms, plus the requirement that several others are present to some extent for a particular period of time, perhaps for two out of the last four weeks. In some cases the clinician is even guided with respect to symptoms that should *not* be present (i.e. their presence indicates that a particular diagnosis should not be made).

For simplicity, only the DSM will be described here, as this deals specifically with mental illness. However, both will be referred to, where appropriate, when we then critically assess the validity of categorising mental illnesses.

The DSM axes

Later versions of the DSM have been improved with the introduction of a **multi-axial format**. DSM IV has five axes, although a diagnosis can be made from information gathered from Axes 1 and 2 alone. The additional three axes allow for the 'fleshing out' of the full diagnostic picture:

- Axis 1 lists the major types of illness (see Table 2.1). These are very similar to the classifications of ICD 10.
- Axis 2 covers enduring (lifelong) conditions including mental handicap and personality disorders. The former needs no further clarification. The latter are a cluster of disorders including paranoid, schizoid, anti-social and narcissistic personality disorders, in which sufferers show lifelong patterns of maladaptive behaviour.
- Axis 3 permits identification of underlying medical conditions which may affect mental function – for example, hyperthyroidism (overactivity of the thyroid gland), which mimics certain features of mania.
- Axis 4 codes for psychosocial problems that a person might be experiencing, and which may have an effect on the disorder.
- Axis 5 requires an assessment of the current level of adaptive functioning (in simple terms, the extent to which an individual's mental state is interfering with their day-to-day life).

Table 2.1 Axis 1 categories

- Disorders first diagnosed in infancy/childhood/adolescence: for example, learning and developmental disorders, attention deficit and hyperactivity, autism.
- Delirium, dementia, amnesia, etc.: these disorders usually take us to the other end of the age-scale, and encompass serious and often irreversible impairments of cognition and mental function.
- Substance-related disorders: ingestion of one or more of a variety of substances (LSD, alcohol, etc.) is deemed to have brought about the change in mental functioning.
- Schizophrenia and other psychotic disorders: marked to a greater or lesser extent by the presence of delusions (false beliefs), hallucinations (false perceptions) and disordered thinking. The individual's behaviour signals loss of contact with reality, either intermittently or indefinitely.
- Mood disorders: as the name implies, the primary disturbance for this set of disorders is to mood (or affect). It

encompasses various degrees of depression, mania, bipolar disorder (otherwise known as manic-depressive illness) and seasonal affective disorder.

- Anxiety disorders: DSM identifies ten different types, including phobias, obsessive-compulsive disorder and post-traumatic stress disorder.
- Somatoform and dissociative disorders: in the former, the individual repeatedly complains of physical symptoms which have no basis in reality. In the latter, there are sudden inexplicable changes to memory or consciousness (again, in the absence of any physical causes).
- Sexual- and gender-identity disorders: sexual dysfunction disorders. The paraphilias, fetishism, paedophilia and sado-masochism are amongst those listed.
- Eating and sleeping disorders: the former identifies anorexia and bulimia; the latter encompasses a range of sleep disorders including insomnia, narcolepsy and sleep apnoea.
- Factitious disorder: this rare diagnosis applies to people who deliberately induce physical or psychological symptoms apparently in order to gain attention.
- Adjustment disorders: this refers to the development of an emotional or behavioural disorder, clearly related to some major life stressor, not meeting any other Axis 1 diagnosis.
- Impulse control disorders: the name is self-defining. This controversial diagnostic category includes kleptomania, pyromania and even pathological gambling.

Criticisms of ICD and DSM

The strengths and weaknesses of classification in general are considered elsewhere in this series. Here we restrict ourselves to a brief consideration of some problems related to classification systems such as the DSM and ICD. Criticisms tend to focus on the issues of reliability or validity, and to question the general suitability of a categorical as opposed to a dimensional approach.

Reliability

In simple terms, reliability is concerned with the extent to which there is agreement about a diagnosis. Early versions of DSM (I and II) were criticised because reliability was disappointingly low, even for major categories of mental disorders. However, both DSM IV and ICD 10 can boast significant improvements in reliability. One of the most recent inter-rater reliability studies, conducted by Sartorius *et al.* (1993), just prior to the publication of ICD 10, demonstrated very good reliability for the diagnosis of schizophrenia, mood disorders and anxiety disorders. However, agreement about subtypes of disorder (which type of schizophrenia a person is suffering from, for example) often showed a much lower level of reliability. From this and other similar studies, it would seem that while the major categories of mental disorder can be reliably identified, there is further scope for improving the reliability of diagnosis of subtypes of disorder.

Validity

In this setting, validity is really about the extent to which there is merit in distinguishing diagnosis A from diagnosis B, C or D. Researchers recognise at least three different forms of validity. *Aetiological* validity means that the same causes should be found in all people in a particular diagnostic group. So, for example, if anxiety is caused by X, Y and Z, then other people with X, Y and Z might also suffer from anxiety. *Concurrent* validity means that people with the same diagnosis should share some other features not used in the diagnosis. *Predictive* validity means that members of the same diagnostic group can expect a similar course of illness and have a predictable outcome or response to treatment.

In psychopathology, the extent to which each type of validity is achieved varies widely. Since we do not know the causes of most mental disorders, aetiological validity is usually impossible to establish. Researchers have had better success in providing examples of concurrent validity: the marked memory impairment found in people with schizophrenia (Stirling, Hellewell *et al.* 1997) would be one example. Clear examples of predictive validity include the favourable response of people with bipolar disorder to the drug lithium and the poor outlook for people who develop schizophrenia at an early age and who have predominantly negative symptoms (see Chapter 3).

Categorical versus dimensional approaches

DSM and ICD are both categorical systems, in which mental illnesses are seen as discrete diagnostic entities. Supporters of the alternative *dimensional* approach argue that most symptoms of mental disorder are essentially exaggerations of the range of feelings and emotions that we all experience; that the distinction between normal and abnormal is a matter of degree and that it can be arbitrary. So, for example, the disturbance in mood experienced by the person with depressive illness might be regarded as simply a more pronounced form of the low mood that we all sometimes suffer. In general, we are in agreement with the dimensional approach. However, although clinicians may, from time to time, disagree about whether or not a particular individual has crossed the line into mental illness, the blurring of boundaries does not, in our view, invalidate the distinction between severe mental illness and 'normality'. (See our discussion of 'hearing voices' in Chapter 12.) Besides, even a dimensional approach requires some form of clinical judgement to be made about whether or not a particular individual would benefit from treatment. Also, it is worth noting that, with categorical systems such as DSM and ICD, the operational criteria actually require dimensional judgements to be made. Take, for example, the subtype of phobias in the Axis 1 category of anxiety disorders. Here we are required to make a dimensional judgement in deciding whether or not the fear of, say, spiders is severe enough to be classified as a phobia.

Finally, we should note that it is much more important for a person to receive the appropriate treatment than the appropriate diagnostic label, although we are also aware that the two (diagnostic label and treatment) are closely linked.

List three advantages and three problems associated with adopting a classification system such as the DSM.

Progress exercise

Paradigms of scientific psychopathology

In this book we emphasise the merits of a scientific approach to studying abnormal behaviour. In defence of this approach, it is often claimed that science is uniquely objective. However, a moment's thought indicates that this cannot be so: scientific study is carried out by people who bring to the work their own perspectives. They set the research questions, the hypotheses to be tested, the methods used and they interpret the data. In short, science is not and arguably never can be *entirely* objective.

In psychopathology, we recognise the existence of several different schools of thought or orientation, referred to by the philosopher Kuhn (1962) as paradigms. A *paradigm* is a conceptual framework or approach within which a scientist works. For example, just as a **Freudian** would probably be uninterested in the search for genetic markers for mental illness, a neuropsychiatrist might be indifferent to the content of dreams. The former may favour a **case study** method, while the latter may prefer random assignation to experimental and control groups.

According to Kuhn, the important thing is to realise that most people operate within a particular paradigm which will influence the way they think about mental illness, the way they research it and the treatments that they advocate. It is better to recognise this at the outset, than to pretend that scientific psychopathology is an entirely objective domain, unaffected by the prejudices of the people involved.

In the realm of psychopathology, five paradigms are usually identified. For the time being it is sufficient to note that the biological

Table 2.2 Paradigms of psychopathology

biological paradigm

key idea	abnormal behaviour results from faulty brain functioning
interest in	behavioural genetics, neurotransmitters, structural brain abnormalities
treatments	drugs, ECT, psycho-surgery
comment	the dominant paradigm, but tends to ignore psychological factors

learning paradigm

key idea	abnormal behaviour (like normal behaviour) is learned
interest in	operant and classical conditioning, reinforced dysfunctional behaviours
treatments	systematic desensitisation, modelling, token economy
comment	weak on explaining causes, but has generated many effective treatments
key idea	abnormal behaviour develops from 'irrational' patterns of thinking

cognitive paradigm

interest in	dysfunctional thinking, negative schema
treatments	cognitive (behavioural) therapy, rational emotive therapy
comment	weak on explaining causes, but cognitive therapy may have widespread applications

psychoanalytic paradigm

key idea	abnormal behaviour results from unresolved childhood experiences
interest in	repression, unconscious conflicts

treatments	psychoanalysis, insight oriented and brief psychotherapy
comment	inherently appealing but generally unsupported theory

humanist and existential paradigm

key idea	the uniqueness of the individual and their need for 'self-actualisation'
interest in	free will, personal experience and development
treatments	counselling, insight therapy, group therapy
comment	hard to evaluate because it lacks rigour and is not susceptible to scientific analysis

paradigm is the natural successor to somatogenesis, while the learning, cognitive, psychoanalytic and humanist paradigms focus on different aspects of psychogenesis. Some of the key features of each paradigm are identified in Table 2.2.

Crossing boundaries in psychopathology

We suggested earlier that people who worked in the field of psychopathology tended to identify with a particular paradigm. However, in recent years practitioners have gradually become more willing to move beyond the boundaries of their own preferred paradigm and adopt procedures from other paradigms *if they seem to work*.

To some extent, this trend towards **eclecticism** is a response to the expression of dissatisfaction from clients/patients. For example, the depressed patient may indicate that although ECT has improved their mood, something further, such as counselling or cognitive therapy, would be welcomed to bring about a sustained recovery, or help deal with the social pressures of everyday life. (See the case study of Mary in Chapter 6.)

However, it is the scientific evidence from recent comparative studies that brought about most interest in eclecticism. We review one such – Elkin *et al.*'s 1985 NIMH study on treatments for depression – in Chapter 13. Elkin and her colleagues showed that three distinct therapies, namely drug treatment, cognitive therapy, and inter-personal psychotherapy, *all* led to a greater improvement in mood in depressed patients than did placebo. Other recent studies have shown that combinations of therapies are sometimes clearly more effective than individual treatments alone. Teasdale *et al.* (1984), for example, showed that depressed patients made a faster recovery and were less likely to become ill again if they completed a course of cognitive therapy *in addition* to receiving antidepressant medication. These studies force clinicians to look beyond their own viewpoint, and adopt a more pragmatic approach to treatment.

Progress exercise

For each paradigm list the major strengths and weaknesses, and identify one form of treatment that follows from it.

Summary

The ICD and DSM have been developed as internationally applicable systems for the classification of disorders. Recent versions of each, which overlap considerably, make use of operational criteria to aid effective diagnosis. Though widely adopted, both have often been crit-icised for lacking reliability and validity and for their use of a categorical approach.

The biological paradigm has developed from the principle of somatogenesis. The learning, cognitive, psychoanalytic and humanist paradigms emphasise different aspects of psychogenesis. The eclectic approach encourages the use of treatments, individually or in combi-nation, from different paradigms.

Further reading

Holmes, D. (1998) *The Essence of Abnormal Behaviour*, London: Prentice Hall Europe. An up-to-date review of the field of abnormal psychology targeted at undergraduate level. Very readable, with an excellent and detailed section covering paradigms.

Barraclough, J. and Gill, D. (1996) *Hughes' Outline of Modern Psychiatry*, 4th edn, London: Wiley. A pocket guide to psychiatry. Chapters on different disorders have similar headings, making the text easy to follow. Includes a very interesting chapter on the Mental Health Act, and is generally strong on treatments.

The nature of schizophrenia

Introduction

Schizophrenia will affect about one person in a hundred at some time in their lives. It is a **psychotic disorder**, in that contact with reality and insight are impaired. However, there is great variability between individuals in the symptoms experienced and in their responses to these. In this chapter we consider the main features and the different subtypes of schizophrenia.

Clinical picture

Schizophrenia is an *episodic* illness, in which periods of disturbance are usually interspersed with periods of better (more normal) functioning. In an acute flare-up of schizophrenia, patients may have great difficulty distinguishing between their inner experiences and external reality. There may also be profound disturbances of thinking and perception. Symptoms commonly encountered in acute schizophrenia include the following:

(a) *Hallucinations.* Hallucinations are perceptions that have no basis in external reality, but which are nevertheless perceived as coming from an external source. Auditory hallucinations, in the form of voices, are most commonly encountered, although other senses, including vision, smell, or even taste, can also be involved. The person may hear voices discussing them or commenting upon their thoughts and actions, often in a derogatory or abusive manner. Unsurprisingly, the sudden onset of hallucinations is often associated with great fear and anxiety, although occasionally patients find the voices they hear helpful or even comforting. Some patients, for example, converse with, or shout back at their voices, while others may sit as if they are listening to them.

(b) *Delusions.* Delusions are fixed, false beliefs, not shared by others from the same cultural or educational background. Delusions of persecution are common, with patients perhaps maintaining that they are being pursued by secret agents from a foreign country. Delusions of power and greatness (grandiose delusions), or with a religious content, are also frequent and there is often a pronounced pseudo-philosophical theme. Concerns about the need for mass re-education, or the establishment of world government, for example, are not untypical. Often, particularly in established illness, a complex web of delusional ideas is evident.

(c) *Passivity phenomena.* This intriguing cluster of symptoms is characterised by a person believing that their thoughts or actions are initiated not by them but by an external (and usually bad or harmful) force. Some patients are able to exercise a degree of control over such impulses; others act on them but claim that the impulse to do so had not been their own! Commonly patients develop delusional explanations for passivity experiences, involving occult forces, hidden transmitters or extra-terrestrials.

(d) *Interference with thoughts.* Patients with schizophrenia often experience interference with their thoughts, which they may again attribute to an external force. In the case of *thought inser-*

tion, the individual has the sense that thoughts or ideas are, somehow, being planted in their mind. In contrast, patients with *thought withdrawal* experience their thoughts being abruptly taken (snatched) from their minds. *Thought broadcasting* is the experience that thoughts are radiating out from their mind and can be 'picked up' by other people.

Other symptoms frequently found in schizophrenia, but not generally regarded as diagnostically significant, include the following:

(a) *Lack of insight.* Many patients show a reduced awareness of their condition. In extreme cases, poor insight may lead an individual to the view that their hallucinations, delusions and other symptoms are entirely real.

(b) *Movement abnormalities.* Disturbances in movement are seen occasionally in schizophrenia. Rarely these take the form of catatonic features, as described below.

(c) *Abnormalities in the expression of emotion.* Many patients with schizophrenia show abnormalities in affect (the expression of emotion). In extreme cases, the emotions displayed may be completely inappropriate to the situation (for example, they may laugh on hearing bad news). Sometimes, patients appear to be emotionally distanced or removed from others, and their emotions are dulled; this is known as having *blunted affect*.

(d) *Mood symptoms.* Depressive symptoms may affect up to one third of patients at any one time. Elation is also occasionally seen. About one in eight patients who meet the diagnostic criteria for schizophrenia also meet the criteria for major affective disorder. The term **schizo-affective disorder** is used to describe illnesses of this sort.

(e) *Language abnormalities.* The speech of people with schizophrenia may seem illogical, with abrupt or obscure shifts between one theme and the next, a feature referred to by clinicians as *knight's move thinking* (a reference to the unusual move of this chess piece). In rare cases, the speech can be so jumbled as to merit the description of *word salad*. Patients may also sometimes use neologisms (invented words) to describe concepts of importance to them.

(f) *Lack of drive.* Patients often show a lack of drive or initiative and a diminished interest in the outside world. This is usually more apparent in the later, chronic stages of the illness, but can be present early on.

(g) *Intellectual impairment.* Many people with schizophrenia have difficulties with learning and memory, and in their ability to plan or make use of information. Deficits can be extremely severe, with some patients being unable to recall even the most basic items of personal information, such as their date of birth. Cognitive deficits appear to be present in the early stages of schizophrenia, although whether or not there is further deterioration over the course of the illness remains a matter of dispute.

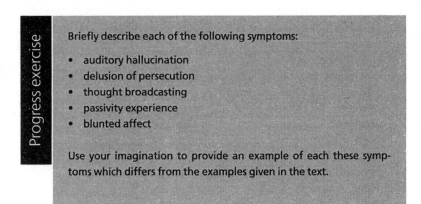

Progress exercise

Briefly describe each of the following symptoms:

- auditory hallucination
- delusion of persecution
- thought broadcasting
- passivity experience
- blunted affect

Use your imagination to provide an example of each these symptoms which differs from the examples given in the text.

Onset

The onset of schizophrenia typically occurs in late adolescence or early adulthood, although onset in later life is seen occasionally. Onset in childhood is rare. The emergence of hallucinations and delusions is often preceded by a period of weeks or months in which low mood, anxiety, bewilderment or other changes in affect are seen. Individuals may become isolated from family and friends and may encounter difficulties in concentration and attendance at work and school. This gradual build-up of symptoms sometimes makes it difficult to identify with any clarity precisely when the illness began.

Course

Traditionally, it was assumed that the typical course of schizophrenia was one of progressive deterioration. The expectation was that, over the course of the illness, hallucinations and delusions might become much less prominent, but that the individual would be left with deficits in intellect, drive and personality (the so-called *defect state*). Today many patients can expect to have a much better outcome than this. One of the best studies of the course of schizophrenia was by Shepherd, Watt *et al.* (1989), in which the outlook for patients was summarised as follows:

- Approximately one in five patients will have only one **acute episode**, will return to their previous level of functioning and will have no lasting impairment.
- Approximately one-third of patients will experience several acute episodes, but there will be full recovery and little lasting impairment.
- A further one in ten patients will also have several acute episodes, with either continued symptoms or a lasting but stable level of impairment, and will not return to previous levels of functioning.
- About one third of patients will have several acute episodes, each of which will be associated with an increasing level of impairment and with no return to previous levels of functioning.

Factors associated with good outcome

Although predicting outcome is an imprecise art, patients who are married, or who have good educational or work records seem to do better. Females have a better outcome than males. A better outcome is also associated with an acute, or sudden, onset of illness, particularly one which follows a clear stressor or precipitant and in which **positive symptoms** (described below) are most apparent. In addition, if a patient's first episode of illness is brief (lasting a month or less) and they respond well to drugs and recover completely, then their long-term outcome is better. Interestingly, the International Pilot Study on Schizophrenia (IPSS) – which is described more fully in the research reviews in Chapter 13 – indicated that the outcome of schizophrenia may be better in developing countries than it is in the industrialised world.

27

Factors associated with poor outcome

A poor outcome is predicted by an early and progressive onset, poor social and educational adjustment, and the presence of **negative symptoms** (described shortly). The use of illicit drugs, such as cannabis, also appears to worsen the outlook for patients and seems, in particular, to be associated with a higher risk of relapse.

Finally, there is now convincing evidence from recent research that the chances of a good long-term outcome in schizophrenia are improved if patients' symptoms are treated promptly. Conversely, a long delay between the onset of symptoms and the start of medication usually results in a slower recovery from the initial episode and a poorer long-term outcome.

Epidemiology

Schizophrenia appears to affect all cultures and racial groups from around the world. The IPSS demonstrated that schizophrenia occurs *with similar frequency* in all of the countries involved (an observation which, incidentally, poses difficulties for anyone arguing that social or family factors are of sole importance in the development of the condition). As we mentioned earlier, the likelihood that a person will develop schizophrenia in their lifetime is about 1 per cent, although the rate of occurrence of new cases is quite low, at about 2–4 per 10,000 population per year (0.02–0.04 per cent per year).

The risk of *developing* schizophrenia is similar in all socio-economic groups, although there are more sufferers in the lower social classes and in deprived urban areas. At one time social psychologists thought that the inner-city urban environment directly caused schizophrenia in some people. However, research has shown that the over-representation of sufferers in these groups is related to the effects of the illness on the ability of patients to work. The large number of patients in the inner cities can be explained by the movement of sufferers to less affluent areas, where accommodation is cheaper and where there may be more opportunities for casual work.

Subtypes of schizophrenia

As we have seen, the symptoms, course and outcome of schizophrenia show great variability. This has given rise to the view that schizophrenia is not a single illness, but a group of illnesses with somewhat differing aetiologies and natural histories, yet some similarities in symptoms.

Over the years, there have been many attempts to divide schizophrenia into smaller groupings, none of which has been completely successful. The major problem has been that the subgroupings themselves are not stable over time, with patients moving from one category to another and back again. Another problem is that most of the classifications are based on symptoms, yet patients very often show symptoms from more than one category. However, despite these limitations, some classifications do have value, particularly as a way of describing a patient's illness at a particular moment in time. Some of the major categories used are described below.

Four subtypes

A long-standing classification of schizophrenic illnesses, adopted by earlier versions of the DSM, divides symptoms into the following subtypes:

(a) *Paranoid schizophrenia*, which is marked by sudden onset, with prominent hallucinations and delusions, often with a persecutory theme.
(b) *Hebephrenic schizophrenia*, which is characterised by early onset and gradual progression, with disturbances of thinking, affect and behaviour, in addition to hallucinations and delusions. Some patients may show unpredictable or irresponsible behaviour.
(c) *Catatonic schizophrenia*, which is seldom seen today. It involves characteristic disturbances of movement. Awkward or seemingly uncomfortable postures are assumed and may be held for many hours. Patients may fall into *catatonic stupor*, in which, despite remaining fully conscious, they lie motionless and apparently unaware of their surroundings.
(d) *Simple schizophrenia*, which is characterised by a progressive deterioration in personality, involving dulling of emotions

(blunted affect) and loss of drive, but without hallucinations or delusions.

Positive and negative symptoms

The features of schizophrenia can be divided into positive symptoms, which might be thought of as reflecting an excess or distortion of normal function, and negative symptoms, representing a decrease or loss of normal function. In this scheme, proposed by Crow (1980), hallucinations, delusions and passivity phenomena are positive symptoms, while a loss of drive and the blunting of affect would be classified as negative symptoms. As we have mentioned, this is a classification of symptoms, rather than of patients, many of whom show differing combinations of positive and negative symptoms during the course of their illness.

The three syndrome model

Liddle (1987) used the powerful statistical technique of factor analysis to examine how the symptoms of schizophrenia could be grouped on the basis of their tendency to cluster together. Three sets of symptoms were identified: those related to *reality distortion* (hallucinations, delusions); those related to *disorganisation* (chaotic behaviour, disorders of thought and speech, inappropriate affect) and those related to *poverty* of ideas and movement (corresponding broadly to negative symptoms). In additional studies, using psychological tests of brain function and sophisticated brain-imaging techniques, Liddle has shown that each of these symptom groups or **syndromes** may be linked to disturbed activity in a specific brain region. However, it would be wrong to conclude from this that there are three distinct varieties of schizophrenia, as most patients over time show varying degrees of the symptoms from all three syndromes.

Two phases of illness

Perhaps, in clinical practice, the most useful classification of patients is into the two stages of illness: the *acute* and the *chronic*. The acute phase, which may last for many years, is characterised by positive symptoms and disturbance of behaviour, while the later chronic phase is characterised by under-activity, reduced motivation and flattening of emotional responsiveness. These two stages of illness are illustrated in the following case studies.

Case study 1: Acute schizophrenia

Simon, 20, lived at home with his parents. Over recent months, his parents had become concerned about his behaviour. He had lost contact with his friends and was becoming increasingly reclusive, remaining in his room and eating alone. He could be heard in his room talking to himself for long periods, at times in an agitated manner. He would seldom leave the house during the day, but would occasionally venture out in the early hours of the morning.

His parents became more worried and feared he might be taking drugs. They decided to call the doctor when they found that he had scratched the words 'good' and 'evil' on his arms, along with other unusual symbols. The GP visited the house and found an unkempt-looking but polite young man, who denied having any problems. The GP was, however, sufficiently concerned to ask the consultant psychiatrist to visit.

When visited at home by the psychiatrist, Simon at first pretended to be out. After some negotiation, he agreed to let the psychiatrist in. Simon was, at first, very suspicious and denied that there was a problem. Eventually, he told the psychiatrist that he had become very worried about all the evil in the world, and that he had discovered he could tell whether people were good or evil, just by looking at them. He described receiving messages from the TV and radio, but would not go into detail.

The psychiatrist was concerned to learn that when he had left the house at night, he went in search of evil people, believing that it was his duty to fight them. Simon's language was difficult to follow, and it seemed as if he may have had other concerns or experiences that he was not revealing. Simon was uneasy about allowing the psychiatrist to look into his bedroom, but did so.

He had painted the walls black, taped the curtains closed and had covered the walls with crucifixes and mystical symbols. There was a large knife near the bed, which, Simon explained, he took with him at night, in case he was confronted by evil people.

The psychiatrist suspected that Simon was suffering from a serious mental illness. The preoccupation with evil, the readiness to fight with evil people and the carrying of a knife were particularly worrying features.

Simon was asked if he would be willing to be admitted to the in-patient unit of the local hospital, for a period of assessment. However, he refused, saying that he did not need help. The psychiatrist was sufficiently concerned about the possible risks that he arranged for an approved social worker to visit, so that Simon could be admitted to hospital under an Assessment Order (Section 2) of the **Mental Health Act**.

Following admission, it became clear that Simon's thinking was dominated by ideas of good and evil. He believed that the forces of evil were taking over the world and were recruiting people to carry out evil deeds on their behalf. He felt personally under attack by the forces of evil: the principle evidence for this being a strange prickling sensation he had in his scalp and some howling noises that he could hear.

In hospital, he was at first unwilling to engage in any activities and instead sat alone, either on his bed or in a corner. His reluctance to use the lounge stemmed partly from his belief that the TV and radio were sending him messages. He said that one particular newsreader was evil and that she would send him messages and put thoughts in his mind. He said that she and others could exercise control over his body and related an instance when he had felt that she made him drink a cup of tea, which he had not wanted to do.

For the first few weeks, Simon claimed that he was not ill and that he did not need treatment. The psychiatrist made the diagnosis of schizophrenia and a few days after admission, prescribed the antipsychotic medication, haloperidol, given by tablet. Simon showed a gradual improvement over the first month of treatment. He became progressively less concerned with his ideas of good and evil and began to spend more time with other patients and staff. The occupational therapist arranged for him to take part in a daily schedule of creative activities, at first working alone, but later as part of a larger group.

After six weeks in hospital, Simon seemed much better. He could watch TV and said that his previous concerns now seemed quite incomprehensible to him. He said that he no longer felt that his thoughts or actions were being interfered with. He still heard the howling noises, but these were no longer a source of worry to him. His parents, also, were aware of the improvement and said that Simon was more sociable and relaxed than he had been in many months. After a few 'trial periods', during which Simon lived at home with his parents, attending the hospital during the day, Simon was discharged home. For the next few weeks he continued to attend the activities organised by the occupational therapist, but later switched to attend the pottery class at the local day centre.

Simon was advised that he would need to continue on his prescribed medication for quite some time and was offered monthly appointments with the psychiatrist and a community psychiatric nurse. One year later, he had remained well.

Case study 2: Chronic schizophrenia

Frank, 58, had been a patient in the local mental hospital for many years. About three years ago, the hospital had been closed and he had been discharged to live in a shared house, along with four other former patients.

Frank was diagnosed as having schizophrenia. For as long as he could remember, he had heard voices, which took the form of people discussing his actions and sometimes commenting on what he was about to do. Usually Frank didn't mind the voices, although at times they would become abusive towards him and he would shout back at them. Frank recalled that, every so often, a new psychiatrist would suggest that he change his medication, to try to stop the voices. Frank, however, was quite content with the medication he was taking, which was a three-weekly injection given by the community psychiatric nurse. He was against any change, as he had learned from experience that this seldom seemed to do any good and might even give him side-effects.

Frank currently has few activities. He seems to have no friends and no contact with his family. He tends to sit in the lounge, watching television and smoking and he has little motivation to leave the house. He tends not to cook or wash his clothes, but he likes to go to the shops with his care worker, who visits every two days and who helps him to cook a meal. About twice per week, the care worker takes Frank to the local day centre, where he can listen to records and drink tea with other patients. He tends not to talk to the other patients, but doesn't mind going if he is taken by his carer.

Frank shows many of the features of chronic schizophrenia. He still has auditory hallucinations, but they no longer appear to be a source of concern to him. The main problems are in his lack of drive and motivation and his inability to care independently for himself. While a number of these problems may, in part, reflect many years of institutionalisation in the mental hospital, Frank nonetheless shows marked negative symptoms.

Treatment

People with schizophrenia are almost always treated with **antipsychotic medication**. There are many such drugs, all of which appear to work by interfering with one of the brain's chemical messengers, dopamine. These drugs are referred to as *dopamine antagonists*

1 See Kevin Silber's book in this series, *The Physiological Basis of Behaviour*, for more information on neurotransmission and drug action.

because they tend to lessen activity in this **neurotransmitter system**.[1] In addition, some drugs interfere with other neurotransmitters such as serotonin (5-HT) and histamine. These actions probably contribute both to their effectiveness and to their side-effects. Use of antipsychotic drugs, otherwise known as the neuroleptics or major tranquillizers, usually results in an improvement in the symptoms of acute psychosis. Taken for prolonged periods, they also protect against further relapses (Crow *et al*. 1986; Curson *et al*. 1985).

Recently, there has been renewed interest in psychological treatments for schizophrenia. These are used alongside medication – a wide range of psychological therapies are now being established in clinical practice. Working with a cognitive-behavioural therapist (who is usually a clinical psychologist), some patients can develop techniques to gain control of their hallucinations and delusional ideas. There is great interest at present in the use of cognitive behavioural therapy (CBT) for patients in their first episode of illness. Research suggests that long-term outcome may be improved if treatment is started early enough. A recent evaluation of CBT by Kuipers *et al*. (1998) demonstrated not only the effectiveness of the treatment, but also that the benefits were still evident nine months after treatment had finished.

Other psychological approaches include *social skills training*, in which patients are helped, through role-play, tuition and experience, to acquire new social skills and consolidate existing ones. When patients live with relatives who are particularly critical of them, *family therapy* can reduce risk of relapse. In this procedure, the family and a therapist meet regularly, so that concerns can be aired, open communication can be encouraged, and skills to avert conflict acquired.

Summary

Schizophrenia is a serious mental illness, affecting approximately one per cent of the population and occurring with similar frequency in all countries and cultures. It is an episodic illness and there is great variability in the eventual outcome. The symptoms of schizophrenia are also variable, but can be thought of as occurring under three headings: symptoms of *reality distortion* (such as hallucinations, delusions, thought broadcasting), symptoms reflecting *disorganisation* (chaotic behaviour, thought disorder, emotional incongruity) and *poverty* symptoms (loss of drive, social withdrawal). Although antipsychotic

Go back to the case study of Simon. As you re-read this account, try to decide which symptoms are being described. From a moral and civil liberties perspective, do you think the psychiatrist was justified in his actions?

drugs are the most likely form of treatment, psychological procedures such as cognitive behavioural therapy and family therapy appear also to be of value, if used alongside conventional medication.

Further reading

McKenna, P.J. (1994) *Schizophrenia and Related Syndromes*, Oxford and New York: Oxford University Press. An outstanding and very detailed review of almost all the conceptual issues, clinical concerns and research approaches related to schizophrenia.

Frith, C.D. (1992) *The Cognitive Neuropsychology of Schizophrenia*, Hove: Laurence Erlbaum. A comprehensive review of neuropsychological research in schizophrenia, with an excellent summary of his own theory of what causes the symptoms of schizophrenia.

4

Aetiology
of schizophrenia

Introduction
Biological approaches
Psychological approaches
Summary

Introduction

In view of the nature of schizophrenia, the wide range of theories about its cause should come as no surprise. Somatogenic approaches have focused on the role of genetic factors and have concentrated on identifying abnormalities in brain structure and function. Psychogenic approaches have emphasised the effects of adverse childhood experiences, particularly abnormalities in family interactions, in the aetiology of the disorder. A recent approach in family-oriented research has been to test the link between family tension (measured by expressed emotion) and recurrence of illness following recovery from the acute episode. Another relatively new approach examines the roles of cognitive and neuropsychological abnormalities in the development of particular symptoms.

Biological approaches

Genetic factors

There is overwhelming evidence that genetic mechanisms influence the propensity to develop schizophrenia. This evidence comes from four types of research: family pedigree studies, adoption studies, twin studies and large-scale **gene**-mapping studies.

Family pedigree studies　These studies involve the assessment of hundreds of people from extended families in which more than one person has schizophrenia. By identifying all of the people with schizophrenia and working out how they are related to one another, we can draw conclusions about how the illness may be inherited. Pedigree studies demonstrate that the risk of developing schizophrenia increases the more closely one is related to someone who already has the illness. First degree relatives, such as children or siblings of patients, have about a 10 per cent risk, first cousins about a 3 per cent risk, and second cousins under 2 per cent (which is not much greater than the risk to members of the general population, of about 1 per cent). (See Slater and Cowie 1971; Kendler *et al.* 1994.)

These studies have been criticised because they fail to take account of the shared environment: after all, closely related people tend to live together. However, were genetic mechanisms not involved, it is hard to see why cousins, aunts and uncles should have a three-fold greater risk, when they usually live away from the person with schizophrenia. Therefore, in general, pedigree studies have provided supportive, but not conclusive, evidence for the role of genetic factors.

Adoption studies　A second approach to understanding the contribution of genetic mechanisms is to study people who have been adopted. One approach is to study the adopted-away children of people with schizophrenia. If there were no genetic factors involved, then we would expect that the risk of developing schizophrenia would be much less in those children who were adopted away than in children who continue to live in the same household as their affected parent(s). In fact, Heston (1966) and Rosenthal (1971) have shown that there is the *same* risk to children who have been adopted away from the affected parent, which is strong evidence for the operation of a genetic mechanism.

There have also been studies of the children of healthy people who were adopted by parents who themselves had schizophrenia (e.g. Wender *et al.* 1974). We might expect to see a higher than average risk of schizophrenia in these children, if it was related to the conditions in the home environment; on the other hand, if genetic factors were important, then we would predict that adoption by ill parents should not increase risk. Wender's data supports the latter hypothesis, indicating that growing up in proximity to someone with schizophrenia is not in itself a significant risk factor for the later development of the illness.

Twin studies   This research relies on the fact that **monozygotic twins** (MZ, or identical twins) are genetically identical, while **dizygotic twins** (DZ, or non-identical twins), like ordinary brothers and sisters, share on average only 50 per cent of their genetic make-up. First of all, we should say that twins are no more likely to develop schizophrenia than anyone else. However, if the development of schizophrenia were due to genetic factors, we would expect a higher rate of **concordance**, or similarity, for schizophrenia in MZ twins than in DZ twins, if one twin was already affected. If genetic factors were not important, then the concordance rate for schizophrenia would be no higher in MZ twins than for siblings generally. The available data suggest that having an MZ twin with schizophrenia is one of the highest risk factors for schizophrenia of all: 48 per cent of all co-twins are also affected. The corresponding rate in DZ twins is only 10 per cent, which is about the same as for siblings generally (Gottesman and Shields 1972).

While twin studies provide strong evidence for the operation of genetic mechanisms, they also indicate that other, non-genetic, factors must be important. If schizophrenia were a wholly genetic disorder, we could expect a concordance rate of 100 per cent in MZ pairs in whom one twin was already affected. But, as we have seen, the real rate is less than 50 per cent, which indicates that additional factors must be involved, either to increase the vulnerability of the affected twin or to protect, in some way, the healthy twin.

Gene-mapping studies   Some researchers claim to have found evidence for specific genes that seem to be associated with schizophrenia. One example is the study by Sherrington *et al.* (1988). Using a form of genetic fingerprinting technique and working with a small number of extended families in which several members were known to have schizophrenia, this group provided evidence of a link between schizophrenia and a gene located on **chromosome** 5. This study generated considerable interest and other research groups set out to determine whether this same association could be found in families that they were studying (e.g. Kennedy *et al.* 1988). So far, however, other researchers have not been able to replicate the finding, suggesting that Sherrington's observations were either a 'false positive' result (a sort of statistical fluke), or were limited to the particular families in his study.

In summary, there is convincing evidence that genetic mechanisms are important in the development of schizophrenia. Beyond this, we do not know on which chromosomes the responsible genes are located, nor how the genes influence the emergence of symptoms. Genes alone do not *determine* who will develop the illness, they merely influence the *probability* of doing so. Interestingly, only about one third of patients with schizophrenia have a close relative with the illness. It might be tempting to interpret this as a sign that there are two forms of schizophrenia, one that is inherited and a second that is not. However, this does not necessarily follow. If schizophrenia were due to the action of a number of genes and each gene individually had only a small effect, then we would expect this pattern. Many people might have a few of the genes that might lead to schizophrenia, but there may be only a small number of people who have inherited a sufficient number to put them at serious risk of developing the illness. The result would be exactly what we find – i.e. some patients with a number of affected relatives but many more having no detectable family history.

Brain structure and schizophrenia

Studies using the techniques of computed tomography (CT) and magnetic resonance imaging (MRI) have shown that, in comparison with normal people, people with schizophrenia have smaller brains and larger cerebral ventricles (the fluid-filled cavities within the brain). The differences are small, but have been found in many studies (e.g. Raz and Raz 1990). Post-mortem studies have also revealed evidence of subtle disturbances in the structure and organisation of brain cells, particularly in the regions of the temporal and frontal lobes.

These findings naturally raise the question of cause and effect. One possibility is that abnormalities in brain structure reflect the *effects* of the disease process, or of the medication used in treatment, rather than the underlying *cause*. While we cannot discount this possibility completely, the subtle changes in brain structure described above are actually more consistent with an abnormality in the development of the nervous system. Indeed Murray *et al.* (1988) has proposed that schizophrenia is, in fact, a neuro-developmental disorder. In other words, an illness in which the brain has grown abnormally during early development. The post-mortem data is also consistent with this possibility. Many of the leading schizophrenia researchers today are particularly interested in this proposal.

In support of the idea of abnormal brain development, there is evidence that people with schizophrenia show abnormalities in behaviour and social interaction many years before the onset of obvious symptoms. The parents of people with schizophrenia, for example, commonly recall that, as children, their offspring had difficulties with language, emotions and relationships with others. Recently, researchers have studied the school reports of people who later developed schizophrenia, drawing similar conclusions (e.g. Jones *et al.* 1994). One group has even made ratings of the behaviour of pre-schizophrenic children, using their parents' home movies. Once again, results offer evidence of a lifelong pattern of abnormal cognitive and emotional development (Walker *et al.* 1993).

What might have caused these abnormalities in brain structure? One possibility is that they may have a genetic basis. Another is that they may result from subtle brain damage. It has been suggested that problems in pregnancy and delivery may lead to anoxia (oxygen starvation) and thereby to brain damage. For example, patients with schizophrenia have been found to have had a greater than expected number of pregnancy and birth complications such as oxygen starvation at birth or breech delivery (baby delivered bottom first) (Lewis and Murray 1987). However, the importance of these factors in the development of schizophrenia is still unclear, as some follow-up studies have failed to show any marked excess of birth complications in patients with the illness (e.g. McCreadie *et al.* 1992; Done *et al.* 1991).

A further possibility is that the brain abnormalities seen in schizophrenia are due to a viral infection contracted early on in child development, perhaps even before birth. A finding consistent with this idea is that people with schizophrenia tend to be more likely to have been born during the winter months. Some researchers have investigated whether schizophrenia is more common in people born during influenza epidemics, when a large proportion of the population become infected with flu. The balance of evidence is that exposure of the mother to flu, especially in the middle months of pregnancy, does appear to increase the later risk of schizophrenia, although the effect is relatively modest (Bar *et al.* 1990). Some studies have failed to show this effect at all (Crow *et al.* 1991; Torrey *et al.* 1992).

In 1983, Crow suggested that schizophrenia may result from infection with a **retrovirus**. These infectious agents are transmitted between people, particularly those in close contact with one another. By incorporating themselves into human DNA, they can then be passed from one generation to the next. Crow's proposal provided an explanation for the situation in which individuals with no family history of schizophrenia develop the illness and then seem to pass it on to their offspring. Although this appeared to be an attractive hypothesis, there is no firm evidence that would suggest a role for retroviruses in the development of schizophrenia. This proposal has, in fact, never been widely accepted and Crow has himself moved on to propose an *evolutionary* theory of schizophrenia. He now proposes that the origins of schizophrenia can be traced back to the process of brain specialisation that occurred as primitive man began to develop sophisticated language skills (Crow 1997).[1]

Brain function and schizophrenia

Researchers have studied brain function using techniques such as positron emission tomography (PET) and functional MRI (*f*MRI).

---

1 See John Stirling's book *Cortical Functions* (in this series for more information on brain hemispheric specialisation.

This is an evolving area of research, but preliminary evidence shows that the symptoms of schizophrenia reflect disturbed function within specific brain regions (e.g. McGuire *et al.* 1993).

Attention has focused on the brain's neurotransmitter systems. **Neurotransmitters** are the chemical messengers that allow brain cells to communicate with each other. The human brain makes use of several hundred different neurotransmitters, but the most important as far as schizophrenia is concerned is dopamine.

In its simplest form, the *dopamine hypothesis of schizophrenia* proposes that symptoms arise because of over-activity within the dopamine system. Two pieces of evidence support this idea. The first, as we mentioned in the previous chapter, is that all antipsychotic drugs tend to *lessen the activity* in the dopamine system by blocking (literally occupying and disabling) one particular type of dopamine receptor (known as the D_2 receptor). Put another way, all drugs with D_2 blocking effects tend to improve the symptoms of schizophrenia (Seeman 1980). Conversely, drugs that boost dopamine function, like amphetamine or L-DOPA, tend to make schizophrenic illnesses worse, or to bring out symptoms closely resembling those seen in schizophrenia in otherwise healthy people.

These observations provide circumstantial, yet consistent, evidence that dopamine is implicated in schizophrenia. Since the theory was first formulated by Snyder (1976), many studies have examined these issues in more detail. For example, researchers have used PET to measure the number of dopamine receptors in the brains of people with schizophrenia, when alive and after death. Although several studies have provided evidence of dopamine over-activity (Reynolds 1989), some have failed to do so. The picture is complicated by the fact that antipsychotic medicines also bring about long-term changes to dopamine receptors. A handful of studies have overcome this problem by recruiting subjects who have never taken drugs. Wong *et al.* (1986), for example, examined drug-free patients and showed a two- to three-fold increase in the number of dopamine receptors in several brain regions.

Although the dopamine hypothesis has gained some support from research, many important questions remain. At the moment, we cannot easily explain how abnormalities in the dopamine system lead to the *differing* symptoms of schizophrenia. The fact that the illness is characterised by periods of disturbance interspersed with episodes of normality also presents problems for the dopamine hypothesis. It is probably unlikely that a disorder as varied as schizophrenia could arise from an abnormality of just one neurotransmitter. Researchers are currently exploring how dopamine interacts with other neurotransmitters in the brain, such as serotonin and glutamate. However, there can be little doubt that dopamine will be involved when the precise role of neurotransmitters in schizophrenia is eventually clarified.

Progress exercise

(a) Summarise in separate short paragraphs the four lines of research evidence in support of a genetic basis to schizophrenia.

(b) Based on the material you have read so far, which of these approaches provides the strongest evidence and why?

(c) Why do genetic researchers know (from their work) that non-genetic factors must also contribute to the development of schizophrenia?

Psychological approaches

Psychodynamic explanations

There have been several attempts to explain the development of schizophrenia from a psychodynamic perspective. Freud (1896) thought that the symptoms of schizophrenia arose because of inner conflicts. The argument went as follows. An individual may have a wish or impulse (such as a homosexual urge) that is in some way unacceptable to them. By the process of **projection**, the person unknowingly displaces these views on to someone else and then behaves as if the impulse originated with the other person, and was being directed towards them. In this way, Freud reasoned, rather than admitting to their own homosexual urges, individuals might develop paranoid ideas that other people wish to persecute them. Unfortunately, Freud never actually tested this proposal and there is no research evidence that would support these ideas.

Other psychodynamic writers such as Jung (1939) and Sullivan (1924) argued that major psychological stresses result in the **regression** of an individual to an earlier stage of psychological development. If the stresses continue, there would be the risk that the coping mechanisms would become overwhelmed, leading to the emergence of schizophrenic symptoms. Like most psychodynamic explanations, supportive evidence is absent, and few if any researchers have tested these proposals experimentally. However, the core idea is that stressful events precipitate schizophrenic breakdown, and many patients' illnesses do appear to start following major stresses, such as examinations or the ending of a relationship. A number of researchers have looked at life events and schizophrenia, but the results are not clearcut; Bebbington *et al.* (1993), for example, reported that schizophrenic breakdown was *not* linked with an excess of stressful life events in the preceding months.

Family theories

Other commentators have suggested that schizophrenia is a way of thinking and behaving acquired in childhood, usually as a result of the attitudes, communication and behaviour of parents. Fromm-Reichmann (1948) coined the term *schizophrenogenic mother*, to describe a parent who was cold, domineering and manipulative, and who had a marked tendency to induce conflict in others around her. According to Fromm-Reichmann, this combination of characteristics made these mothers unable to show normal affection to their children. She considered that this deficiency in mothering caused the child to develop a lifelong distrust and resentfulness towards others and thereby to go on to develop schizophrenia.

Bateson *et al.* (1956) argued that schizophrenia develops as a result of repeated exposure to what he called the *double-bind*. By this term he was describing communications that are inherently contradictory or conflicting, and which put the child in a 'no win' situation. For example, a child would be in a double-bind if he were told by his parents to go outside and play football in a muddy garden, but also that he must not get his clothing dirty. The child would have no opportunity to please his parents, as all of the actions open to him would be likely to lead to parental disapproval.

Lidz *et al.* (1958) suggested that abnormalities in the relationships between the parents of schizophrenic patients were primarily responsible for their developing schizophrenia. He coined the terms *skew* and *schism* to describe such relationships. *Skew* describes a marriage where one partner is dominant and the other submissive, while *schism* describes the relationship in which parents are emotionally distant from one another. He proposed that, over a period of time, these dysfunctional patterns of interaction would be psychologically harmful to the child, leading ultimately to their developing schizophrenia.

Laing (1971) put forward similar ideas, once going so far as to say that schizophrenia was a sane response to a disordered environment. According to Laing, abnormalities in relationships within the family, together with abnormal communication between parent and child, undermine the child's sense of self. Laing also suggested that the development of schizophrenia in one member of a dysfunctional family might help to relieve pressures on other family members. According to Laing, the affected child thereby functions in some way as a sort of scapegoat or sacrifice.

There is little, if any, scientific support for most of these ideas. There is no evidence whatsoever that shows mothers of patients to be aloof, cold or rejecting, or that people with schizophrenia were repeatedly exposed to double-binds as children. Indeed, when researchers have measured deviant communication in families where children have schizophrenia, results indicate that patterns of parental communication are no different to those observed in parents of non-patients (Liem 1974). Over-concern or anxiety are frequently observed in parents, but this may just as easily be explained as being a consequence of living with someone with schizophrenia, than as being the cause of illness (Stirling 1994).

Expressed emotion (EE)

In contrast to the efforts reviewed in the previous section, one line of psychosocial research *has* provided convincing evidence of how different patterns of family interaction may affect outcome of schizophrenia and, in particular, the tendency of patients to have further episodes of illness. According to Vaughn and Leff (1976), EE is a term used to describe the criticism and negative feelings that are sometimes expressed by the relatives of patients towards the person with schizophrenia. Regardless of symptoms, people recovering from schizophrenia who live in high-EE households tend to relapse more frequently than those living in low-EE households (Stirling *et al*. 1993). There seems to be an exposure effect, as more contact (in other words, more hours per week spent together) increases the risk of relapse. However, antipsychotic medication seems to have the opposite effect, protecting against the harmful influence of high levels of EE.

Using this information, psychologists have developed a form of family therapy, in which high-EE relatives are shown ways to reduce levels of expressed emotion. Evidence from these *intervention studies* shows that family therapy, targeted at high-EE families, can lead to significant reductions in rate of relapse (Hogarty *et al*. 1991). The therapy includes practical help and information, troubleshooting tricks and stress-reduction methods.

The cognitive-neuropsychological approach

Recently, there has been interest in the possibility that some of the symptoms of schizophrenia may be related to abnormalities in specific mental functions, such as memory and awareness. This approach has the dual advantages of being rooted in the techniques of experimental psychology and being amenable to scientific evaluation.

The psychologist Frith has suggested (1992) that *passivity symptoms* (see Chapter 3) arise because the individual fails to monitor effectively their own thoughts, impulses and actions. Because of this, the patient's own thoughts and ideas are not recognised as their own but are misattributed to the outside world, giving rise, for example, to the symptom of thought insertion. Delusions of control and auditory hallucinations may occur in a similar way: an individual may plan some speech, but if it is not 'flagged' as being self-generated, it may be interpreted as an auditory hallucination. One implication of this research is that there must be designated brain-areas that monitor plans and intentions. Spence *et al*. (1997), using PET, have identified such an area in the left frontal lobe of the brain, and have shown that this area is under-active in patients with passivity symptoms.

(a) To what did the following writers attribute the cause of schizophrenia:

   Bateson; Fromm-Reichman; Lidz; Laing; Snyder; Crow; Gottesman and Shields; Frith.

(b) List four reasons why somatic explanations of the basis of schizophrenia are currently favoured by researchers and clinicians in this area.

Review exercise

Summary

Family, twin and adoption studies have demonstrated that vulnerability to developing schizophrenia is influenced by genetic factors, although additional influences seem necessary to translate this predisposition into illness. These influences may be psychological (e.g. stressful life events) or environmental (e.g. brain damage following viral infection or birth complications). There is now good evidence that psychotic symptoms arise because of abnormalities in brain function, as these abnormalities are detectable by both neuropsychological tests and brain-imaging. Attempts to explain the development of schizophrenia purely in terms of disturbed patterns of family communication have generally not been successful. However, expressed emotion (EE) research has shown that the long-term course of illness can be modified both by biological factors (antipsychotic medication) and social factors (less contact with high-EE environments, or intervention to reduce levels of EE among household members). The neuropsychological approach demonstrates that many of the symptoms of schizophrenia can be understood as arising from problems in self-monitoring.

Further reading

Kalat, J.W. (1998) *Biological Psychology*, 6th edn, Pacific Grove: Brooks Cole. The standard undergraduate biopsychology text. Beautifully illustrated, easy to read and up-to-date. Chapter 16 covers severe mental illness from the physiological perspective.

Gottesman, I.I. (1991) *Schizophrenia Genesis*, Oxford: Freeman. Easy-to-read review of genetics research in schizophrenia, with many personal anecdotes.

5

The nature of affective disorders

Introduction

Most people will be aware of a day-to-day variation in their mood and that of the people around them. You might have experienced short periods of feeling miserable, perhaps at times of stress or personal disappointment, or a few days of elation following particularly good news such as success in examinations. The broader term *affect* is used to describe not just the subjective aspects of mood, but also to include features that are evident to the external observer, such as the person's behaviour and speech. Therefore *mood* or *affective* disorders are characterised by disturbances of affect, in the directions of depression or elation. These illnesses are distinguished from the normal variation in mood on the basis of two criteria:

(a) *Degree of disturbance.* There is a profound disturbance in mood, in either the direction of depression or elation, which is out of proportion with the circumstances.
(b) *Duration.* The changes persist for weeks – or even months – and appear largely unresponsive to changes in situation.

Depression

The central feature of the depressive illness is a persistent lowering of mood, although many other symptoms may also be present. Sufferers may have disorders of thinking, attention and concentration, feelings of anxiety and disturbances in sleep and appetite.

Over the years, a variety of terms have been used to describe different aspects of the depressive illness. Depression which seems to follow an obvious stressor, such as redundancy or bereavement, is sometimes described as *reactive*. In contrast, the term *endogenous*, which literally means 'arising from within' is used to describe illnesses which do not appear to be related to stressful events. Minor illnesses are sometimes referred to as *neurotic* disorders, while the term *psychotic* is used to describe a more severe illness, in which the sufferer may have obvious disturbances of thinking and perception.

Clinically, it *is* useful to distinguish between minor and major (or severe) depressive states, and this distinction can be seen in both DSM IV and ICD 10. However, it is important to remember that there is no clear dividing line between depressive illnesses of differing severity, and attempts to demonstrate separable forms in community samples have usually failed (see Paykel and Hollyman 1984).

Major depressive illness: the clinical picture

(a) *Mood symptoms*

There is a severe and persistent lowering of mood. Patients are likely to describe themselves as feeling profoundly sad. Although mood is typically flat, some patients show a predictable change in mood through the day, known as **diurnal mood variation**: mood is particularly low first thing in the morning, but improves some-what as the day goes on. Some patients may also experience high levels of anxiety.

(b) *Speech, thinking and suicide*

Depressed mood can affect a patient's speech, which may seem slow and monotonous. These abnormalities are likely to reflect thinking, which will typically be pessimistic and gloomy. Thinking, in turn, can be distorted by marked feelings of guilt. In severe disorders, this can be reflected in the development of delu-sions, in which patients ruminate over past misdeeds (real or imagined), blaming themselves for their misfortunes or those of others.

Ideas of suicide are common in depressive illnesses. These may range from a vague sentiment that things would be better if the patient were to die, to a fully formed plan to kill themselves. About one in eight patients ultimately take their own lives.

(c) *Perceptual abnormalities*

In severe states, abnormalities of perception may occur. Hallucinations are consistent with the prevailing mood and may, for example, take the form of voices abusing or criticising the patient.

(d) *Somatic or bodily symptoms*

So-called **biological symptoms** of depression are very common, and indicate a disorder that is of moderate severity or greater. *Sleep* may be affected by early morning wakening. Complaints of *lethargy* are common. *Appetite* is usually greatly reduced and patients may have marked weight loss. Occasionally patients eat excessively, which perhaps represents comfort-eating. A reduced interest in *sexual activity* is also common. Many depressed patients show an increased concern with bodily illness and hypochondriacal complaints are common.

(e) *Effects on behaviour*

A lack of enjoyment is typical and patients may describe an inability to derive pleasure from activities or interactions with others. This symptom, referred to as **anhedonia**, may lead patients to lose interest in themselves, their appearance, their work or their home.

Some patients are unable to be still for any length of time, and pace about incessantly, often wringing their hands in anguish (the so-called 'agitated depression'), while the behaviour of other patients is retarded, or slowed.

The following case study is typical of the pattern of behavioural changes that are seen in someone suffering from major depression.

Case study 1: Major depression

Mike, 45, is a manager of a large company. He has a reputation at work of being very organised, effective and demanding of the best from his colleagues. He has always been a good mixer and he has a wide circle of friends, both within the company and at home. He lives with his wife and three teenage children.

Over recent months, following the news that his father has lung cancer, Mike has become withdrawn and moody. He has noticed a complete loss of interest in both his work and his home, such that he seems no longer to enjoy dealing with problems at work, nor to enjoy meetings with his friends. He has found it increasingly difficult to maintain concentration on his work and has found himself becoming indecisive and vague. Mike has begun to worry that he has 'lost his edge' and he is ashamed to think that his colleagues may have come to that view as well.

Mike's wife and children, too, are concerned about him. He would always previously want to hear from his children about their activities and would often want to advise on their homework; now he seems no longer to want to spend any time with the family. He sits in a chair in the lounge watching TV, but he doesn't seem to take any interest. He no longer talks with his wife and over the last few months has not shown any interest in sex.

Previously always of immaculate appearance, Mike seems to have stopped worrying about his clothes and, for the last week, he has worn the same shirt and tie.

One day, Mike finds he just has no energy to go to work, he feels worn out and unable to face leaving the home. He becomes tearful and tells his wife he feels he has let her down and that he is a complete failure.

At the doctor's, Mike recounts his problems of the past few months. It transpires that he has been waking every morning with great anxiety at about 3 or 4 AM. Sometimes he has lain awake for hours wishing he were dead; recently, he has begun to think about taking an overdose or killing himself with the car's exhaust fumes. His mood shows diurnal variation, in that there is a progressive easing through the day, followed relentlessly by extremely low mood the following morning. He has not been eating during the day and seems to have lost quite a lot of weight, as his clothes are now quite loose. He is convinced that he is a failure and that he has let down his wife and family. He describes anhedonia, or a pervasive lack of enjoyment or pleasure, and says that he can recall no enjoyable activities over the past few months.

The doctor starts Mike on an antidepressant medication. In view of the ideas of suicide he suggests that perhaps referral to a psychiatrist for admission as an in-patient is necessary. Mike is opposed to this and says that he will call at once if he feels at all inclined to harm himself. Mike is relieved to be told that he has a depressive illness and feels much better now that his wife knows what has been going on. Although it feels alien to him, Mike agrees not to go to work for the next few weeks.

Over the coming weeks, Mike's mood steadily improves. He feels less distanced from his family and more able to join in conversation. Progress, he has noted, tends to be uneven: there are some good days, followed by a few bad days, when at times he feels as if he would have been better to kill himself. Generally, though, the bad days are becoming fewer and he feels more ready to meet with his friends again.

After six weeks, Mike is impatient to return to work. He goes to see his boss and the company medical officer and it is agreed that Mike should start in a gradual way, working two days per week. After a few weeks, Mike feels ready to undertake more responsibility and so returns to work on a full-time basis. He continues to take the antidepressants, having been told by his doctor that he will need to do so for at least the next six months.

Comment Mike experienced an episode of major depressive illness. He showed a clear change from his previous personality, with a marked lowering of mood, together with disturbances in sleeping, appetite, social and occupational functioning. As is often the case, Mike persevered with his job for several weeks, despite increasing problems. He has responded well to treatment, and the outlook is good.

Minor depressive states: the clinical picture

As we said earlier, there is no clear dividing line between the major or severe depressive illnesses and milder forms. Patients with less severe depression experience low mood, but this is neither so pronounced nor so unresponsive to changes in situation as it is in the major illness. Sleeping, appetite and the ability to derive pleasure may all be affected, but again the disruption is not as marked as that seen with the more severe disorders.

The predominant symptoms in minor depressive illnesses are usually anxiety and disturbed sleep. This contrasts with the more severe states, where the clinical picture is dominated by feelings of hopelessness and resignation. For some people, depression may persist for many months or even years, yet never be particularly marked. This less severe but enduring type of depression is called **dysthymia**.

Seasonal affective disorder (SAD) is the name given to a less severe form of depression, in which low mood develops in the autumn, persists throughout the winter and improves in the spring. People with SAD seem sensitive to seasonal changes in the intensity and duration of daylight. It has been suggested that this brings on depression by altering the function of a region of the brain called the hypothalamus. Interestingly, patients with SAD often find that their symptoms improve following a treatment known as **phototherapy**, in which they look at a bright light-source for approximately two hours each day.

Mood disorders associated with childbirth

(a) *Baby blues*

Low mood and tearfulness occur in 30–50 per cent of women in the first few days after childbirth. Known colloquially as the 'baby blues', this transient disturbance of mood requires no specific treatment, other than general reassurance and support.

(b) *Postnatal depression*

About 1 in 10 women develop postnatal depression, which is similar in degree to depressive illnesses occurring at other times, although concerns about parenting skills and the health of the baby are common. Postnatal depression usually responds well to antidepressant medication and psychological support.

(c) *Puerperal psychosis*

Following giving birth, about 1 in 500 women develops the much more serious condition of puerperal psychosis. This resembles major depression, as described above, but there may also be symptoms more typical of schizophrenia and mania. There is often a clear risk of suicide. The child too might be in danger because of the mother's delusional symptoms. She may, for example, believe the baby has magical powers and is sending messages to her, or controlling her movements. Puerperal psychosis nevertheless responds well to treatment.

Mania: the clinical pic

The central features of mania are a markedly elevated mood and an inappropriate sense of well-being. Manic illnesses tend to be recurrent, with acute episodes lasting, if untreated, for several weeks, interspersed with extended periods of normality.

(a) *Mood symptoms*

Typically the mood is elevated and expansive, with patients feeling optimistic and over-confident about themselves and their abilities. Some patients, though elated, exhibit a marked irritability and have a tendency to express an extreme and inappropriate anger, or even aggression, towards others.

(b) *Abnormalities in thought and speech*

The manic patient's speech is typically rapid, and difficult to interrupt (a feature known as *pressure of speech*). They may describe great plans for the future, which are fanciful and incompletely thought through. The topic of speech may jump abruptly from one subject to another, with little logical connection (so-called *flight of ideas*). The changes in speech seem to reflect an increase in the rate of thinking, which patients often describe in terms of thoughts flooding into their minds.

(c) *Psychotic symptoms*

Patients may have delusions, usually consistent with their prevailing mood. They may, for example, be convinced that they have great physical or mental powers, or that they must carry out some important role for the benefit of others. The delusions often relate to the patient's normal personality and lifestyle: someone interested in sport, for example, may form the belief that they are one of the greatest athletes of all time. Hallucinations, such as voices, may also be evident. Again, these are usually consistent with the dominant mood.

(d) *Effects on behaviour*

The over-activity and disturbed thinking seen in mania frequently lead people to act on their beliefs and impulses. Patients may sleep only briefly, if at all, engaging in various hectic activities as soon as they wake. Few of these will be completed before the next task is undertaken. Self-care and normal daily responsibilities are very often neglected. Occasionally mania is associated with increased sex drive. There may be aggression and violence directed towards others; suicide and self-harm also occur. The combination of impaired judgement, lack of insight and increased drive often necessitates admission to a hospital ward. Unfortunately, patients with mania frequently resist hospital admission during an acute episode and they may have to be admitted against their will, using the powers of the Mental Health Act.

Hypomania

Hypomania is essentially a less severe form of mania. There is no rigid demarcation between the two states, although in hypomania delusions of power and grandeur are absent, as are the extremes of disturbed behaviour. Like manic patients, those with hypomania usually require supervision.

Bipolar affective disorder

This is a diagnostic term from the DSM classification system. It is used to describe the illnesses of patients who have had *both* manic and depressive episodes (hence the alternative name, *manic depressive illness*). The term implies that mania and depression are polar opposites, representing the two ends of a spectrum of mood disorder.

> (a) Explain what is meant by the term 'affect'.
> (b) What are the two criteria by which affective disorders are distinguished from normal variability in mood?

Progress exercise

Case study 2: Hypomania in a patient with bipolar affective disorder

Ron became worried when his wife, Sandra, started to complain about the decoration in the living room. She had already called the decorators and planned to replace the colours with something much brighter. She was quite insistent and was exasperated by her husband's suggestion that this was not necessary.

Over the past twelve years, Ron had seen his wife develop several previous hypomanic episodes. There tended to be a characteristic pattern. She would appear dissatisfied with the decoration of the house or with her car, or perhaps with her career, and would begin to make changes. At first she might engage in some repainting or might visit car showrooms looking for a better car, but very often, things would deteriorate rapidly. On one occasion she removed the old wallpaper and spent hundreds of pounds on new paper, in garish and bright colours that she would not usually have chosen. Another time she booked herself and the family on a holiday to the Seychelles, without telling anyone, and it was only when Ron saw the credit-card statement that he learned what had happened. Sandra had been admitted to hospital with hypomania on three occasions. There had also been an episode in which Sandra had become severely depressed, which occurred soon after she had had an episode of mania. For the past two years Sandra had been taking her lithium on a daily basis, and it seemed that this had been effective in reducing both the frequency and the intensity of her mood-swings.

Ron contacted Sandra's community psychiatric nurse and asked her to visit. The CPN found Sandra to be excessively cheerful, to be laughing uproariously for no obvious reason and to be complaining that her husband would not let her out to do some shopping. She was wearing very bright clothes, and had several different silk scarves tied around her head. Sandra did not accept that she was at all unwell.

After discussion with Sandra's doctor, it was agreed that

Sandra should attend the psychiatric day hospital, as an alternative to the in-patient unit. Ron agreed to supervise Sandra during the evenings and to go with her to the day hospital every morning. She was started on the antipsychotic medication, haloperidol (given by tablet three times per day), and the lithium was continued. (Ron suspected that his wife had not been taking her lithium for about a week or so prior to becoming unwell.)

Sandra attended the day hospital every day for the next two weeks. At first she had complained loudly about the staff, whom she said were insufficiently senior and who only wanted to suppress her creativity and to keep her cooped up in the day hospital. She was reluctant to sit down for any length of time and tended to interfere with the activities of other patients. After a few days, her mood seemed more settled. She began to engage in activities such as art, and to talk appropriately with patients and staff. By the end of the third week, Sandra was almost back to her normal self; she was sleeping normally and no longer preoccupied with plans to make changes around the house. Sandra attended the day hospital on alternate days for one more week and there appeared to have been no deterioration in her condition. She was then discharged, with an arrangement to be visited at home by the community psychiatric nurse.

Comment   Clearly Sandra had developed a further episode of her affective disorder. She showed elevated mood, together with characteristic changes in confidence, activity and judgement. Delusions and hallucinations were not present, so the correct diagnosis is of hypomania, rather than mania. In view of her previous history, there was clearly a risk that Sandra would act on the basis of her disturbed mood and overconfidence and do something that she might later regret. There was, therefore, a clear need for both close supervision and effective treatment.

Hypomanic patients sometimes require compulsory admission and treatment under the Mental Health Act. However, with the cooperation of relatives, it is sometimes possible to treat patients without the need for hospital admission, as happened in this case.

Epidemiology of the affective disorders

Feelings of depression are common, with up to 20 per cent of the population describing some symptoms at any one time. Symptoms are more frequent among women, the lower socio-economic groups, and divorced and separated people. (See, for example, Brown and Harris 1978.)

Overall, the lifetime risk of major depressive illness is approximately 6 per cent, although this figure varies widely, even within the industrialised world. Once again, major depressive illness is almost twice as common in women as in men. The estimated lifetime risk of mania is approximately 1 per cent, being slightly more common in females than males (Angst 1978). Bipolar disorders occur equally in both sexes.

Treatment

Depressive illness

Most patients with depressive illness respond well to antidepressant drugs, which work by stimulating one or more of the brain's neurotransmitter systems.[1] Many antidepressants are now available, differing in their effects and side-effects. Unfortunately, for most there is a delay, which can run into weeks, before beneficial effects are seen.

In situations where speed of improvement in mood is important, for example in severe retarded depressive states in which the patient's life may be at risk, treatment with electro-convulsive therapy (ECT) may be used. ECT is still a controversial treatment, although rigorous

1   See Kevin Silber's text *The Physiological Basis of Behaviour* (also in this series) for more information on drug actions.

research has demonstrated its effectiveness and relative safety in severe depressive illness. The treatment involves the induction of a brief episode of epileptic activity in the brain. In severe depressive states, the treatment can be effective quite quickly, with patients showing significant recovery within a matter of days. A course of twelve treatments is usually given over a six-week period. ECT is carried out with the patient under general anaesthetic, and following the administration of a drug which relaxes completely the patient's muscles. ECT is then given using specially designed equipment. Although the electric stimulus induces epileptic activity within the brain, the muscle relaxation prevents the usual movements of body and limbs. Short-term side-effects include muscular aches, which arise from the agent used to relax the muscles, and temporary memory loss. Contrary to the popular view, longer term adverse effects are very uncommon (Zervas and Fink 1991).

There are many more options available for the treatment of less severe depressive states. Cognitive-behavioural therapy (CBT), for example, has been shown by Elkin *et al.* (1985) to be as effective in improving symptoms as antidepressants. (We describe this study in Chapter 13.) CBT involves regular meetings with a trained therapist. Working together, the patient and therapist identify persistent patterns of thinking which may contribute to the disorder and suggest alternative strategies for dealing with difficulties. Cognitive behavioural treatment does not prevent the use of antidepressant medication or of other therapies.

Some depressed patients believe that they benefit from regular meetings with counsellors. They may regard this as helpful in providing general support. However, simple counselling (as distinct from more formal psychological treatments such as cognitive therapy) is unlikely to be effective in improving mood in established depressive illness.

ia

Treatment for an acute manic episode usually involves admission to a hospital, where the patient's behaviour can be supervised and medication administered. Antipsychotic medication or lithium, or possibly both, are needed for the control of the acute disturbance, although these drugs may take several weeks to work. Lithium is also taken on a long-term basis and has the effect of stabilising mood in those at risk of bipolar disorder.

Prognosis

Manic episodes tend to be of short duration, perhaps four to six weeks, although there is a tendency towards recurrence and many patients experience six or more episodes during their lifetime, even with treatment.

The duration of a bout of major depression is more uncertain, but is longer than that of the manic episode. The evidence suggests that most episodes of depression will ultimately clear up, although without treatment this process may take several months or even years (Angst 1978). With treatment the time to recovery can be shortened greatly, although there can be a tendency towards early recurrence. Although many patients remain free of depressive illness for sustained periods, most will have more than one episode.

Review exercise

(a) Write an imaginary case summary (or vignette) of a patient with manic depressive (bipolar) disorder, to illustrate the clinical features they may experience at different stages of illness.
(b) To what extent are the symptoms of affective disorder similar to or distinct from those of schizophrenia?

Summary

In this chapter we have identified and described the two major forms of mood disorder: depressive illness and mania. These are disabling disorders which can lead to suicide. Affective disorders are relatively common and both major depression and mania tend to be recurrent conditions. Milder forms of illness tend to be more commonly found in females. Manic disorders affect men and women equally. Both psychological treatments and drugs provide effective treatments for depressive illnesses, although drugs or ECT may be first choice for severe disorders. Manic depressive illnesses often respond well to treatment with lithium.

Further reading

Davison, G.C. and Neale, J.M. (1998) *Abnormal Psychology*, 7th edn, New York: Wiley. Chapter 10 covers mood disorders.

Andreasen, N.C. (1984) *The Broken Brain*, London: Harper & Row. A book covering most severe mental illness, which includes many superb case studies and vignettes.

6

Aetiology of the affective disorders

 Introduction
Psychological approaches
Biological approaches
Summary

Introduction

Biological, psychological and social factors have all been linked to the development of affective disorders. In general, researchers working from a somatogenic viewpoint have tended to concentrate on more severe illness, whereas those interested in social or psychogenic causes have tended to concentrate on the less severe forms. However, as we mentioned in Chapter 5, drawing a line between major and minor illness is to some extent arbitrary.

Research has identified factors that seem to contribute to a lifelong vulnerability to affective disorders. These include:

(a) genetic factors and the influence of early childhood experience,
(b) the response to stress and other psychological mechanisms, and
(c) changes in brain biochemistry that may be linked to mood.

As with schizophrenia, despite their diverse origins the various theories that we consider need not be mutually exclusive. Indeed, for most people with affective disorders, a number of contributory factors can be identified.

Psychological approaches

Early childhood experiences

Psychoanalytic writers have long regarded deprivation of maternal affection in early life as an important factor in the later development of depression. Freud (1917), for example, was impressed by the apparent similarity between mourning and the symptoms of depression, and suggested that they may share the same causes. Just as mourning is associated with loss, by death, so he argued, might depression result from loss of other kinds. He realised that not all depressed patients had experienced *actual* loss, so he proposed that they may instead be experiencing feelings of *symbolic* loss for someone close to them.

Klein (1934) also thought that abnormalities in early development may cause depressive illness in adult life. She argued that an important stage in early infant development is the point at which a child learns to cope with its mother's temporary absence. She suggested that, if the child fails to move smoothly through this phase of development to the next, a permanent vulnerability to depression might ensue.

As is the case with most psychoanalytic ideas, scientific testing is lacking. Nevertheless, while cognitive and behavioural, rather than psychoanalytic, approaches are preferred today, it *is* generally accepted that certain adverse social experiences in early life can predispose some individuals to the later development of depressive illness. This evidence is considered below.

Psychosocial stress factors

Several large-scale studies, such as that of Brown and Harris (1978), have shown that so-called *stressful life events* are commonly reported in the months preceding the onset of depressive illnesses. Events involving *loss*, such as the ending of a relationship or bereavement, seem particularly closely linked to depression. Other researchers have highlighted the role of *threat events*: these are stressful incidents which involve a serious blow to the individual's physical safety, self-confidence and self-esteem, such as burglary or violent assault. Life events may also be important in triggering episodes of mania.

In their 1978 study of women at risk of depression, Brown and Harris demonstrated not only the importance of life events in precipitating depressive illness, but how these influences could be modified by what they termed 'vulnerability factors'. They identified four vulnerability factors, of which the most important by far was the lack of a close, confiding relationship with a partner. This factor alone was as influential as the other factors combined. The other three factors were the loss of the mother before the age of eleven years, having three or more children under fourteen at home and unemployment.

Learned helplessness/hopelessness

Behavioural work with animals first led to the idea that repeated unpleasant experiences, over which an individual has no control, might induce a state of *learned helplessness*. Seligman (1974) subjected dogs to inescapable electric shocks: at first they ran around in a distressed way, but then they seemed to give up and passively accept the painful stimulation. Seligman was impressed by the apparent similarity between their behaviour and the symptoms of depression. Translating this work to the human situation would imply that some people learn to expect that, no matter what they do, their efforts seem to end in failure. It is this sense of helplessness and lack of control that leads to depression.

The learned helplessness theory provides an attractive model for explaining the development of depression. In practice, though, it may be best suited to explain the development of depression in individuals with chronic social difficulties and poor emotional support and who experience major life events (see the case study at the end of this chapter). However, there are difficulties with the theory. One is that patients with severe illnesses tend to blame *themselves* for their problems. This does not sit easily alongside the idea of depressed people feeling helpless.

Like many scientific proposals, the theory of learned helplessness has been modified and reformulated in light of fresh evidence. In 1978, Abramson, Seligman *et al.* introduced the concept of *attribu-*

tion. They proposed that individuals vary in their attributional styles, that is in their tendency to regard experiences as the result of either their own actions or influences from the outside world. According to the attribution model, aversive experiences are not in themselves sufficient to cause depression, rather people become depressed *only* when they attribute aversive events to external and enduring causes.

A more recent revision is the theory of *learned hopelessness* (Metalsky *et al.* 1993). According to this theory people in a state of hopelessness come to expect either that desirable outcomes will not occur, or that undesirable outcomes will occur. They also feel unable to change this situation. This sense of hopelessness then leads on to the development of depression. This is a good example of a stress-diathesis explanation of causality: life events (which act as stressors) interacting with the diatheses (predispositions) to bring about depression. According to the theory there may be several diatheses, in addition to the attributional style described above. One is an expectation that negative life events will have severe negative consequences and a second is having a low self-esteem.

It is too early yet to judge whether or not the hopelessness model is any better at explaining the development of depression than earlier forms of Seligman's theory. However, the theory received support from the work of Lewinsohn *et al.* (1994), who showed that in adolescents a depressive attributional style and low self-esteem *predicted* the onset of depression.

Cognitive factors

A further psychological theory concerned with vulnerability to depression is that proposed by Beck (1987). In essence this 'cognitive' theory suggests that depressed patients feel as they do because their thinking is biased towards negative interpretations. According to Beck, people who go on to develop depression in later life do so because, during childhood and adolescence, they acquired **negative schema**. Schema are the plans, or mental rules, by which we guide our behaviour in specific situations. These negative schema develop as a consequence of various negative experiences such as rejection by peers, criticism from parents or authority figures, or the depressive symptoms of family members. In later life negative schema become activated whenever the individual encounters a situation resembling that in which the schema were originally acquired. Examples of such schema might include the tendency to give up prematurely when faced by opposition, or the inclination to withdraw from stressful interactions with others.

Beck proposes that people who are vulnerable to depression are apt to think in particular self-defeating ways, such that, whatever the evidence, there is a tendency to draw negative conclusions about themselves. Examples of this sort of *cognitive bias* include:

- Drawing arbitrary inferences on the basis of insufficient evidence (e.g. concluding 'The car wouldn't start, therefore I am no good').
- Selective abstraction, which describes focusing on a detail and ignoring important additional evidence (e.g. 'I must be useless at DIY because that nail fell between the floorboards').
- Over-generalisation, that is to say drawing a sweeping conclusion on the basis of trivial evidence (e.g. 'I have a slight temperature, so I probably have an incurable disease').
- Magnification or minimisation. These biases lead people to continuously overstate their shortcomings and under-appreciate their qualities and achievements (e.g. 'My driving instructor must think I am a hopeless driver because he's always telling me to do things').

Beck proposed that the combination of negative schema, together with the patterns of thinking illustrated above, leads to what he terms the **negative triad**: comprising negative views of the self, the world and the future. The negative triad both predisposes the individual to develop depressive symptoms and then, by reinforcing self-critical thinking, maintains the illness.

Beck's theory appears to have 'face validity' in explaining the development of depression and, unlike some other theories, also has the advantage of being testable. In support of this theory, a number of studies have demonstrated that depressed patients *do* think more negatively about themselves and the world than non-depressed individuals. However, researchers have generally failed to demonstrate that depressed individuals adopt the cognitive distortions and biases described above. There is also a lack of evidence that these mechanisms are present in people *before* the onset of depressed mood. Furthermore, there is no good evidence that cognitive distortions and biases actually *cause* the depressed mood. Therefore, despite being an attractive theory, there is a lack of convincing supportive evidence. However, these ideas have contributed to the development of cognitive therapy, and its close relation cognitive behavioural therapy, both of which have widespread applications in the treatment of depression and other psychiatric disorders.

Progress exercise

Identify and describe three ways in which early childhood experience has been linked with the later occurrence of depression.

Biological approaches

Genetic research

A wealth of data suggests that genetic mechanisms influence vulnerability to affective disorders. The evidence is strongest for the major depressive and manic disorders. (See Chapter 4, pp. 38–40, for a fuller description of the types of genetic study that are conducted.) Twin studies show a high concordance rate for MZ (identical) twins and a somewhat lower rate for DZ (non-identical) twins. For manic depressive illness, Price (1968) reported a concordance rate of 68 per cent for MZ twins reared together, 67 per cent for MZ twins reared apart and 23 per cent for DZ twins. The high MZ:DZ ratio strongly suggests the action of genetic mechanisms. Studies of patients with bipolar disorders who were adopted as children demonstrate that their biological parents have a higher rate of affective disorders themselves, while their adoptive parents do not (Mendlewicz and Rainer 1977).

As with schizophrenia, genetic researchers have studied large families, in which a number of people are affected, to search for a link between particular genetic markers and affective disorder. However, the results have been inconsistent. A group from North America, studying members of the Old Order Amish community, reported an association with a site on chromosome 11 (Egeland 1987), although this finding has not been replicated by other groups. For example, Hodgkinson (1987), working with extended families from Iceland, reported negative results.

There have been fewer studies exploring genetic factors in minor depressive states and findings have been mostly negative. Indeed this research suggests that other factors, such as social and environmental influences or psychological mechanisms, may be more centrally involved (McGuffin and Katz 1986).

Taken together, these studies provide strong evidence that genetic factors influence vulnerability to affective disorders, particularly to the more severe illnesses. We do not know, as yet, how genes work to increase the risk of illness. One possibility is that there may be genetically determined differences in the function of the brain's neurotransmitter systems that are involved in mood regulation. The inconsistent results emerging from genetic association studies suggests that there may be several distinct genetic mechanisms, all working to influence risk in different ways.

Neurotransmitter abnormalities

In addition to the genetic studies outlined above, there is evidence that brain function is disturbed in the affective disorders and that these abnormalities are causally important in the development of symptoms.

The *monoamine hypothesis* proposes that depression is due to an abnormality in neurotransmitters of the monoamine group (Sachar and Baron 1978). Like many theories, this has undergone extensive modification over the years. In its earliest form, the theory proposed that depression was caused simply by a shortage of neurotransmitters. Later and more complex elaborations have involved alterations in the number and sensitivity of receptors, as well as other changes. Three monoamine neurotransmitter systems have been implicated. These are noradrenaline, serotonin (or 5-HT) and dopamine.

Taken together, there is strong evidence that neurotransmitters are involved in the affective disorders. The brains of depressed patients who die by suicide have both reduced 5-HT levels and increased numbers of 5-HT receptors. These, and other observations, have led to the proposal that depression is caused by reduced 5-HT activity within the brain. However, while we can be fairly sure that 5-HT is involved, it appears that some abnormalities in 5-HT function persist after clinical recovery from depression. This suggests that other mechanisms must be involved as well (Deakin and Graeff 1991).

There is also evidence that noradrenaline function may be disrupted in depression. Once again the evidence is circumstantial and incomplete. Both ECT (electro-convulsive therapy) and many antidepressant drugs have complex actions on the 5-HT *and* noradrenaline neurotransmitter systems. However, we do not know the mechanisms by which these drugs relieve depression.

In summary, a number of theories have been put forward relating affective states to disturbances of the major monoamine neurotransmitter systems (noradrenaline, 5-HT and dopamine) in the brain. Although neurotransmitter systems do seem to be involved in some way, most of the theories are at present based on oversimplifications of the workings of the brain.

Interest in neurotransmitter systems has tended to obscure the possible contribution of other biological factors, such as **endocrine** (hormonal) abnormalities. Intriguingly, patients with a wide variety of different endocrine disorders display symptoms of affective disorders much more often than would be expected by chance: For example, patients with an under-active thyroid gland often have symptoms of severe depression. The production of many hormones is controlled centrally by a brain region known as the hypothalamus, leading to speculation about possible hypothalamic disturbances in the development of affective disorders.

Review exercise

Match the names and ideas of the following, providing a brief summary of the origin of affective disorders put forward by each:

Freud, Seligman, Beck, Kety
learned helplessness, symbolic loss, low monoamine levels, cognitive biases

nary

As we have seen, there is evidence that biological, psychological and social factors are all important in the development and persistence of affective disorders. It is important to bear in mind that these influences do not represent separate and distinct routes to the development of affective disorders. All of these factors interact and a stress-diathesis model provides the best opportunity for understanding these problems. People vary in their vulnerability to these disorders, some perhaps because of their genetic inheritance, others because of their early life experience and cognitive style. A wide range of influences can act as stressors to convert this vulnerability into illness. These include hormonal changes and life events. Irrespective of causal factors, changes in mood and emotion are likely to reflect changes in neurochemical function within the brain.

Case study 1: Depressive illness in a setting of chronic social difficulties

Mary, a middle-aged woman, had visited her GP four times in the past few months, each time with a variety of bodily aches and pains. The GP knew her and her family well; her husband and sons were heavy drinkers and had spent time in prison for burglary. He had always suspected that Mary's relationship with her husband was punctuated with violent disagreements, although Mary herself had never complained of this.

Today Mary seemed very unhappy. She was tearful and described how she felt she wasn't able to cope with her husband's continuous drinking. For the last few months she had been particularly tense and her sleeping had been disturbed. She had been lying awake until the small hours thinking over her problems. Her friends, she said, had noticed that she was quieter than usual. She herself had been avoiding her friends as she hadn't wanted them to see her so unhappy. Mary had been neglecting her appearance and on questioning,

---

admitted that she had not been eating well and had lost quite a bit of weight.

Mary also admitted that she wanted to end her marriage, but she was worried about how she would cope afterwards. At times she felt very lonely and desperate, and she admitted to wondering whether her problems would be resolved if she were to die. She added, however, that she didn't want to die and that she would never kill herself because of the effect it would have on her daughters and grandchildren.

Although Mary appeared very unhappy, she said that she very much enjoyed spending time with her young grandchildren.

The GP thought that Mary was suffering from a depressive illness. Mood was low and there was evidence of a change in behaviour, weight and sleep.

At first, the GP prescribed an antidepressant medication for Mary. Unfortunately, over the next few months, her symptoms continued, as did her marital difficulties. Following a major disagreement with her husband, Mary began to drink heavily. The GP tried a change of antidepressant, but this too seemed to lead to only a modest improvement.

In view of the chronic social difficulties that Mary faced, the GP referred her to a social worker for practical help and to a counsellor for emotional support. The social worker, in turn, put her in touch with a group for women in a similar situation to her own. Despite her initial reluctance to attend, Mary came to value the opportunity to share her experiences with others. The counsellor provided Mary with an opportunity to discuss her family- and home-life and to examine her feelings, aspirations and worries. Over a period of months, Mary realised that she wanted to separate from her husband and so, working with her counsellor, she gained the necessary confidence. She continued to take medication as she felt that this was contributing to her gradual recovery.

Some months after the separation from her husband, she realised that her mood was more stable and that she was enjoying her life once again.

Comment This account illustrates the interaction between social situation and mood. In this case, chronic marital difficulties appear to have been a major maintaining factor and the separation was helpful in allowing Mary to make a fresh start.

Further reading

Davison, G.C. and Neale, J.M. (1998) *Abnormal Psychology*, 7th edn, New York: Wiley. Chapter 10 covers mood disorders.

Andreasen, N.C. (1984) *The Broken Brain*, London: Harper & Row. A book covering most severe mental illness, which includes many superb case studies and vignettes.

7

The anxiety disorders and obsessional states

Introduction

Virtually everyone has experienced anxiety: at times of uncertainty or stress, for example, or when facing immediate danger. Anxiety has a protective function. It prepares the individual to respond appropriately to threat. Although anxiety is part of normal experience, for some people it can become a chronic and disabling problem. People with anxiety disorders experience anxiety to a degree that is quite disproportionate to any threat posed.

Anxiety is the central feature of all of the disorders described in this chapter. The main differences between the various types of anxiety disorder that we identify are in the course of illness and in the situations in which anxiety becomes prominent. Therefore we begin this chapter with a general description of anxiety and its associated symptoms, before considering specific types of disorder in more detail.

The experience of anxiety

(a) *Psychological symptoms*

Anxiety is usually accompanied by a feeling of great unease, often with a sense of dread and foreboding, or a feeling of impending panic. An individual may feel they are about to die or to lose control of their bodily functions. Occasionally psychological features will be the only signs of anxiety, but it is much more common for anxiety to include somatic (bodily) symptoms too.

(b) *Somatic (bodily) symptoms of anxiety*

The somatic features include increased heart rate, which may be experienced as palpitations, and an increase in the rate of breathing, which is known as *hyperventilation*. This is often experienced by the patient as a tightness in the chest, difficulty breathing or even breathlessness. Hyperventilation leads to marked reductions in the level of carbon dioxide in the blood and because of this, can lead to light-headedness, to feelings of 'pins and needles' or even to painful involuntary muscle contractions affecting the hands and feet, known as *tetany*. Other physical complaints include a dry mouth, or the urge to use the toilet.

Some somatic anxiety symptoms involve increased muscular tension. In the scalp, this is felt as a headache, usually as constriction or pressure, typically affecting the front of the head. Tension in other muscles may be experienced as aching or stiffness, especially in the back or shoulders. Some patients may have a tremor, which interferes with writing or manual tasks.

(c) *Symptoms reflecting increased arousal*

The psychological and somatic symptoms of anxiety are often accompanied by symptoms arising from heightened arousal. Patients may be 'jumpy', unsettled and unable to relax. They may be irritable with those around them. They may have difficulty falling asleep and may be easily startled. Patients may be unable to concentrate, which may, in turn, impair their ability to deal with complex tasks or to function effectively in a work environment.

Anxiety is often regarded, incorrectly, as a minor or perhaps innocuous symptom. However, anxiety disorders can substantially impair an individual's ability to handle the demands of home and work and may thus be a source of considerable distress.

Phobias

The patient with a phobia has an irrational and disproportionate fear of a particular phobic stimulus and will avoid contact with it. The fear and avoidance are sufficient to impair normal everyday functioning.

Often the irrational fear is related to a particular group of stimuli, such as spiders or sharp objects like knives and needles. Sometimes it is related to particular situations, for example social interaction. Whatever the stimulus, the fear is so great and the anxiety provoked so pronounced that individuals often take extreme measures to avoid contact with, or exposure to, the object of their phobia. In many cases, patients are only too well aware that this avoidance of situations is leading to increasingly abnormal behaviour and to a profound restriction in everyday function.

Specific phobias

These conditions involve excessive fears of specific objects or situations e.g. spiders, cats, heights and so on. Established phobias, if untreated, often persist unchanged for many years, although there is often a good response to treatment. Women are affected much more commonly than men. Phobia-like fears are very common in childhood, affecting boys and girls equally. It appears that with maturation, these fears are lost in almost all males and in many females. In a sense, therefore, phobias in adulthood can be seen as representing the continuation of these earlier fears.

Social phobia

Patients with social phobia have fears about meeting or interacting with others, or about eating, drinking or simply being in public. Sufferers appear to be most concerned about interpersonal contacts in a social setting and specifically about the potential risk of personal embarrassment. The situations that appear most stressful are those in which individuals feel themselves to be under observation by others. In contrast to the specific phobias, males are affected as often as females. The onset of the phobia usually happens in adolescence or early adulthood, and without treatment the problem can persist unchanged for many years. Sufferers often attempt to alleviate their anxiety with alcohol or other drugs, and so drug-dependence may become an additional problem.

Agoraphobia and panic disorder

Agoraphobia, literally 'fear of market places', is a misleading term, implying (as it does) that sufferers are simply afraid of open spaces. Although a fear of open spaces does occur in this disorder, the central features are multiple phobic symptoms, together with a generally high level of anxiety. Usually the person feels most fear when they are furthest from home or away from the assistance of a trusted relative.

Most patients with agoraphobia describe *panic attacks*, which are brief but very distressing episodes of extreme anxiety. A panic attack tends to begin abruptly, without warning, yet improve only very gradually. When a panic attack occurs, the individual may find it impossible to resist running for the safety and security of their own home, such can be the intensity. Unsurprisingly, once a patient has experienced a panic attack in a particular environment, they are often very reluctant to return to the same place again.

Agoraphobic patients tend to avoid situations in which they may experience fear. These may include open or closed spaces, travelling on public transport, or crowds. Agoraphobia can be a disabling condition. In its most severe forms, sufferers can be extremely reluctant to leave the home, even for the shortest journeys and even when accompanied by others. Agoraphobia affects women more frequently than men and the symptoms often begin in mid-life. Once established, the symptoms tend to persist for many years.

A related disorder to agoraphobia is *panic disorder*, in which frequent and repeated panic attacks are a prominent feature. The main difference between the two disorders is that patients with panic disorder tend not to show the enduring anxiety, multiple phobic symptoms and marked avoidance that is seen in agoraphobia.

List the symptoms of anxiety under the following headings:

(a) the psychological symptoms of anxiety
(b) the somatic (bodily) symptoms of anxiety
(c) symptoms relating to increased arousal

Describe what is meant by the following terms: panic attack, specific phobia.

Progress exercise

Case study 1: Agoraphobia

Sarah, a woman in her mid-thirties, was shopping for bargains in a crowded department store during the January sales. Without warning and without knowing why, she suddenly felt anxious and faint. She felt unsteady on her feet and could feel her heart pounding within her chest. She was worried that she was about to faint or have a heart attack. She dropped her shopping and rushed straight home. She noticed that her feelings of panic seemed to improve, the nearer to her house she got.

A few days later she decided to go shopping again. On entering the store, she felt herself becoming increasingly anxious. After a few minutes, she had become so anxious that she could barely decide what she should be doing. A shop assistant noticed her and suggested that she should come to the first-aid room. Once there, she noticed her feelings of anxiety and panic becoming worse and she felt particularly embarrassed at all the attention from strangers that she was receiving.

After these two experiences, Sarah avoided going to the large department store again, in case she had another panic attack. Instead she began to do her shopping at smaller shops. Unfortunately, she found it very difficult even to enter these shops without worrying what she might do if she were to have another panic attack and this worry, she noticed, itself led to her feeling anxious.

A few weeks later, she had another panic attack, this time in one of the smaller shops. Once again, she ran out of the shop and back to her home. After this episode, she was very reluctant to go back to the shops. She asked her husband to do the weekly shopping and instead stayed in the house. After a few weeks, her husband suggested that it was her turn to do the shopping again. Sarah became very anxious and tearful at this thought and implored her husband to do the shopping with her.

Over the next few months, Sarah found that she had panic attacks in more and more places. The typical pattern was that she became more anxious the further away from her house she got. Very often she had a panic attack and had to return home immediately; sometimes she returned home before she developed a panic attack. She tried to avoid the places in which she might have a panic attack, but as the months passed, Sarah found that she had restricted more and more of her activities outside the house. She was able to do the shopping, but only if her husband was with her and if they went at a quiet time. She was no longer able to walk alone into the town centre. Some days she found it impossible to leave the house at all. She noticed that she had become dependent on her husband, not just for practical tasks such as shopping, but also for social interaction, as she lost contact with her friends, whom she could no longer leave the house to meet. She believed that her marriage was under strain; her husband, she felt, resented her dependence on him and they began to have frequent arguments.

Comment Sarah showed the typical evolution of agoraphobia. There is clear progression from occasional panic attacks with avoidance to anticipatory anxiety, widespread avoidance and the occurrence of panic attacks in a variety of situations.

Generalised anxiety

In contrast to the anxiety experienced in phobias and panic attacks, which occurs in brief bursts, generalised anxiety occurs in a more continuous and unfocused form. This is sometimes called *free-floating anxiety* and is experienced as a prolonged sense of unease and dread. This disorder is seen in both sexes, but is more common in females. Without treatment, generalised anxiety can continue for many years. Many patients with generalised anxiety also have prominent depressive symptoms and there is a large overlap clinically with depressive illness.

Adjustment reaction

This refers to a brief episode of anxiety and low mood occurring after the experience of a significant stressor, such as witnessing a bank raid or being made redundant. It is often associated with disturbance of sleep and an inability to concentrate. It is a temporary state and will improve completely within a matter of weeks.

Post-traumatic stress disorder (PTSD)

It is quite common to develop symptoms of anxiety and low mood after experiencing a traumatic and distressing event, such as involvement in a major road accident. In most people, this adjustment reaction lasts only a few weeks. In some people, symptoms persist for many months afterwards, while in others symptoms re-emerge after a substantial delay. In either case the person is suffering from post-traumatic stress disorder (PTSD). The symptoms of PTSD fall into three main clusters:

- persistent symptoms of anxiety
- avoidance behaviour
- phenomena, such as intrusive and vivid recollections or disturbed dreams, that reflect the involuntary re-experience of the traumatic event

---

Case study 2: Post-traumatic stress disorder

Frank, 37, works as a taxi driver. About six months ago, when at work, he was involved in an accident in which a stolen car driven by a group of teenagers crashed into his taxi. He vividly remembers seeing the car coming towards him and him trying unsuccessfully to avoid a collision. He remembers the accident as a time of stress because two of the boys were killed and he was tested for alcohol after it.

Although upset by the incident, Frank had, at first, thought he had coped quite well. For the last few months, he has found himself thinking more and more about the accident. Several times a day he finds himself thinking back over the accident in minute detail; he keeps having the mental image of one of the passengers crashing through the windscreen. At these times, it is almost as if he is back at the scene. He can hear the sounds of the car's brakes and of the impact, and can almost smell the other car next to him. He has begun to have nightmares and is having difficulty getting to sleep. Sometimes, to calm himself down, he drinks a glass of whisky. This is also worrying him, as he doesn't want to drive while drunk.

His difficulties are now affecting his work, in that he no longer can bear to drive past the scene of the accident. Sometimes he pretends not to see passengers so he won't have to pick them up.

Comment Frank showed the key symptoms of post-trau-matic stress disorder. He exhibited the intrusive and powerful recollections, the anxiety and the avoidance behaviour. Fortunately, he was referred by his doctor to a clinical psychol-

---

ogist, whom he saw five times as an out-patient. Although talking about the accident at first was very upsetting, he found that the opportunity to describe to the psychologist his recollections and feelings helped him to 'put the accident into perspective' and to return to work normally again.

Obsessive-compulsive disorder (OCD)

This condition is characterised by *obsessional experiences* and *compulsive acts*. *Obsessions* are thoughts or mental images that, although the patient recognises them as their own, seem to enter consciousness against the patient's will. These thoughts are often repellent or unpleasant, and very often people feel a strong urge to resist or to push the thoughts out of their minds. *Compulsions* are rituals that the individual feels compelled to carry out and that briefly have the effect of relieving anxiety. Commonly patients feel they must repeat rituals a specific number of times. Failure to do so results in increased anxiety and the need to begin the ritual once again. Compulsions are often concerned with personal hygiene or contamination, and these may involve the patient washing themselves, or cleaning items, for many hours each day.

Obsessive-compulsive disorder typically begins in early adulthood. Once established, it may persist for many years, with more or less the same severity. Obsessional symptoms generally, and rituals in particular, can be a cause of considerable disruption to a normal daily routine.

Many patients gain benefit from cognitive-behavioural techniques, such as modelling or thought stopping. These methods allow them to acquire a sense of control over their symptoms. In addition, a particular group of antidepressants known as SSRIs (standing for Selective Serotonin Reuptake Inhibitors) appear to be particularly effective in improving symptoms in individuals who have not responded to psychological treatments.

It is interesting to note that at one time obsessive-compulsive disorder was thought to be extremely uncommon, perhaps because affected people tended not to seek treatment. Recently, however, the disorder has been recognised to affect up to 3 per cent of the population at some time in their lives. In addition to patients with OCD, minor obsessional symptoms are common in the general population and particularly in children.

Treatment

Clinical psychologists are centrally involved in the treatment of many patients with anxiety disorders and have developed a range of treatment techniques for dealing with the various conditions. Specific phobias respond well to *systematic desensitisation*, a process in which patients are gradually exposed more and more directly to their phobic object. Where direct physical exposure to the phobic object is impractical (with crocodiles, for example), then the therapy involves the patient imagining progressively greater levels of exposure. Such *exposure techniques*, when combined with *cognitive therapy*, can be used with patients with agoraphobia and social phobias. *Cognitive-behavioural therapy* and *group therapy* may be beneficial in PTSD. Panic disorder and obsessive-compulsive disorders often respond favourably to treatment with *drugs* from the SSRI group. Patients with marked depressive symptoms may benefit from treatment with *antidepressants*.

Summary

Anxiety is a common experience, which some people experience for prolonged periods, or with an intensity that is out of proportion with the situation. When anxiety interferes with normal daily life clinicians describe the person as having an anxiety disorder. There are several different forms of anxiety disorder. Some, such as phobias and PTSD, tend to be focused on specific events, situations or objects. Others are relatively unfocused, generalised anxiety disorder being an example. Obsessive-compulsive disorders can also be included here, as sufferers typically experience high levels of anxiety, which they attempt to control by engaging in ritualistic and repetitive behaviours.

List:

(a) the psychological symptoms of anxiety, and
(b) the somatic symptoms of anxiety.

We have seen that anxiety occurs in a number of different forms, e.g. generalised anxiety, phobic anxiety, anticipatory anxiety and anxiety in the context of OCD. For each of these forms of anxiety write a few sentences, setting out the key features and identifying how this form of anxiety differs from the others.

Review exercise

Further reading

Rachman, S. (1998) *Anxiety*, Hove: Psychology Press. A concise up-to-date review of theories about and research into anxiety disorders, with a strong behavioural slant.

Aetiology of anxiety disorders

Introduction

In this chapter, we consider the different explanations for the causes of anxiety disorders. As with schizophrenia and depression, a variety of both somatogenic and psychogenic theories has been proposed. As each is considered, remember that they are not necessarily mutually exclusive. Indeed, you will see there is good evidence to suggest that a stress-diathesis model, involving the interaction of somatogenic and psychogenic factors, best accounts for the aetiology of anxiety disorders.

Psychological theories

Psychodynamic approaches

Here the main idea is that unconscious mental conflicts, relating to unacceptable sexual or aggressive impulses, are especially important in the development of anxiety. In particular suppressing the wish to do something that one knows one should not do leads to tension. This tension then provides the energy that is expressed as anxiety.

Freud (1909) suggested that phobias develop when anxieties are focused on an object which *symbolises* a conflict that the individual is facing. It follows from this that phobic anxiety cannot be reduced unless the individual is able to resolve the underlying conflict. Freud illustrated this process by reference to 'Little Hans', a boy whose fear of horses prevented him from leaving the house. He suggested that the fear of horses represented the boy's unconscious fear of his father. The conflict arose, he thought, because of the boy's wish to have sexual relations with his mother, knowing that this would anger his father.

These ideas may provide an opportunity to understand the experiences of the individual patient, but supporting evidence is restricted to reports from psychoanalytic interviews with selected patients.

Conditioning theories

Early psychological theories focused on the idea that anxiety was learned, through the process of **classical (Pavlovian) conditioning**. This theory described how individuals might come to associate fear with a neutral stimulus (the conditioned stimulus or CS), so that exposure to the stimulus would cause them to become anxious. Classical conditioning would occur, according to this view, if the neutral stimulus was repeatedly paired closely with another stimulus (the unconditioned stimulus or UCS) that had the effect on the individual of inducing fear (the unconditioned response or UCR). Over time, fear would come to be associated with the CS, rather than just with the UCS. Eventually, presentations of the CS alone would result in the appearance of fear and anxiety (the conditioned response or CR).

To illustrate this mechanism, Watson and Rayner (1920) induced in a young child, 'Little Albert', the fear of a rabbit, by making a loud crashing sound while the child was playing with it. This case is often cited as an example of conditioning a child into developing a phobia (or irrational fear) of a neutral stimulus: the rabbit. Interestingly the conditioned fear in Albert generalised not just to other rabbits but also to pieces of fur, demonstrating that the conditioned fear had been established towards furry objects generally and not just to rabbits.

Despite Watson and Rayner's example, it is not possible to account for the development of all phobias or anxiety states on the basis of uncomplicated aversive conditioning. However, many patients with agoraphobia do report that their illness started with a single panic attack in a public place. It is also often possible to explain their increasing avoidance and disability on the basis of conditioned avoidance and reinforcement by subsequent adverse experiences.

Two-process theory

The two-process theory, first presented by Mowrer (1939), has been used to explain the persistence of phobias and other fears (see Eysenck 1976). According to this theory there are two stages in the development of fears: the first, brought about by classical conditioning, involves the acquisition of the fear; the second process involves **operant conditioning** (in which behaviour that is rewarded or reinforced tends to be repeated). This leads to avoidance of the feared stimulus and thus the persistence and generalisation of the disorder. For example, a child bitten by a dog may acquire a fear of not just of the dog that bit him, but other dogs as well. If the child subsequently avoids contact with all dogs, then there will be no opportunity to encounter friendly dogs which might lead to extinction of the conditioned anxiety.

The development of agoraphobia might also be explained in a similar way. After having a panic attack in a public place, an individual may then begin to avoid places similar to those in which they first developed anxiety. The consequence may be that the person experiences anticipatory anxiety whenever they think about going to these places again. However, by avoiding such places, they tend not to give themselves the opportunity of being in those situations *without* developing a panic attack, and therefore their symptoms persist.

These proposals indicate that phobias may arise by a process of conditioning (learning) and they provide a useful model for understanding how and why disorders might occur. However, while some people with an anxiety disorder do relate its onset to a particular frightening experience, the overwhelming majority do not. Many patients with severe fears of snakes, aeroplanes and heights, for example, can recall no unpleasant experiences with these objects or situations. Thus the avoidance conditioning model does not appear to account for all phobias.

Furthermore, later attempts to replicate Watson and Rayner's experiment and to demonstrate the acquisition of fear via classical conditioning have generally not been successful. In fact there is little experimental evidence that human beings can be conditioned to fear neutral stimuli, even when these are paired repeatedly with aversive stimuli, such as electric shocks (Davison 1968). On balance therefore, the data suggests to us that not all phobias are learned through the mechanisms of classical and operant conditioning. They may be involved in some illnesses, but, for most phobias, other processes must be involved as well.

Preparedness

The simple conditioning model of phobias proposed that these arise because of the random pairing of neutral objects with fear-inducing objects, such that the neutral objects then become associated with anxiety. It was soon realised that the classes of objects to which patients are phobic do not reflect this random pairing. Nor are phobic objects necessarily those which, in the modern world, should be associated with pain or danger. Cats, for example, are often the subject of phobias, while phobias of cars, motorcycles and electricity are very uncommon. Seligman's concept of 'preparedness' (1971) implies that there are certain stimuli to which anxiety is very readily conditioned and only slowly extinguished. These 'prepared' stimuli are those which were probably associated with danger to primitive man (e.g. insects, heights and small animals). These now appear as the object of phobias.

Cognitive approaches

Some psychologists have suggested that certain 'patterns of thinking' may be important in the development of anxiety disorders. Research demonstrates that emotion and cognition are interrelated and each has an influence on the other. People with phobias, for example, seem to be 'tuned in' to the stimuli that elicit their fears. This was illustrated by Burgess (1981). Using a **dichotic listening task** he showed that phobic subjects were more 'sensitive' to phobia-related words than healthy subjects.

Working from the cognitive perspective, Beck and Emery (1985) proposed that anxious people tend to employ *vulnerability schema*. (Schema can be thought of as the plans or rules that we use to guide our behaviour in particular situations.) Healthy people have schema which guide behaviour and response in positive ways. Possessing 'vulnerability schema' makes people interpret situations in terms of the potential harm to them. This causes them to be overly concerned with danger. The weakness of this explanation, of course, is that it is *circular*. It is a redefinition of the behaviour and attitudes of the anxious person, rather than an explanation of why individuals behave in the ways that they do. There is also a lack of evidence that these styles of thinking precede the onset of anxiety, rather than simply accompany it. Unless they precede the anxiety they cannot be clearly identified as a cause.

A variant of the cognitive model relates specifically to the development of panic attacks, rather than to anxiety generally. Clark (1986) has suggested panic occurs as a result of *a vicious circle* in which anxiety leads to physical symptoms. These in turn activate fears of illness and thereby cause more anxiety. For example, a man with anxiety may become aware of his pounding heart. This may suggest to him that he is about to have a heart attack and the fear of this might cause him to become even more anxious. Heart rate may increase yet further, which he may interpret as evidence of serious illness, leading to a further increase in anxiety and so on. Certainly many anxious patients have concerns about their physical health, and the fear that one is dying is commonly described by people with panic attacks. Support for this proposal comes from the finding of Hibbert (1984) that fears about serious physical or mental illness are more frequent in patients with panic attacks than in anxious patients who do not have panic attacks.

In general, psychological explanations for the development of phobias and panic attacks are better developed and have greater apparent validity than psychological explanations for other forms of anxiety. In Chapter 13, we review Sanderson, Rapee *et al.*'s study (1989) illustrating the importance of cognitive factors in the development of panic disorder.

Summarise in one or two sentences how each of the following may help us understand the basis of anxiety:

- psychoanalytic theory
- classical (Pavlovian) conditioning
- operant conditioning
- generalisation
- vulnerability schema

Progress exercise

Biological mechanisms

The role of psychological mechanisms in the development of anxiety disorders does not, of course, preclude a role for biological mechanisms; indeed, psychological mechanisms presumably depend in some way on activity within brain systems.

The evolutionary basis of anxiety

As we have already mentioned, in addition to being a psychiatric symptom, anxiety is a normal human emotion. Using an evolutionary perspective, anxiety might be understood as a protective mechanism, important in guiding the organism away from sources of danger. The symptoms of anxiety can be understood as part of the 'fight or flight' response – preparing the individual to fight with an aggressor or to flee from harm.

Genetic mechanisms

There is some evidence for a genetic vulnerability to anxiety disorders. Relatives of patients with anxiety disorders are themselves at increased risk of anxiety, and the risk appears to be highest for the most severe disorders. In 1969, Slater and Shields examined seventeen pairs of identical (MZ) twins and twenty-eight non-identical (DZ) twin pairs, in which one twin from each pair had been diagnosed as having an anxiety disorder. Of the MZ co-twins, 49 per cent were diagnosed as also having anxiety disorders, while only 4 per cent of the DZ co-twins had an anxiety disorder. Clearly the higher MZ concordance rate suggests the operation of genetic factors. In particular these may be important in determining *vulnerability* to panic attacks, as the relatives of individuals with panic disorder commonly show a tendency to panic attacks themselves.

Neurotransmitter dysfunction

Anxiety disorders have been linked with disturbances in several of the brain's neurotransmitter systems. One proposal is that anxiety represents over-activity of the noradrenaline neurotransmitter system. Panic attacks can, for example, be induced in healthy people if they are given the drug *yohimbine*. This drug has the effect of increasing noradrenaline neurotransmission and this may be how panic attacks are generated.

An alternative proposal, linking anxiety to disturbances in the serotonin (5-HT) system has been put forward by Deakin and Graeff (1991). Their idea is that the serotonin neurotransmitter system has evolved over millions of years to take responsibility for controlling an organism's response in situations involving danger and stress. One part of the system deals with adaptation to on-going stress. Another part is concerned with situations in which danger is imminent. According to Deakin and Graeff's theory, generalised anxiety arises when the adaptation system is overwhelmed, while panic results from inappropriate activation of the 'immediate danger' system. Thus panic involves activation of the 'fight or flight' mechanism. This is a relatively new theory and has not yet been extensively tested. However, neurotransmitter systems are much more complicated than these models suggest, so it seems likely that further refinements of the theory will be needed.

A stress-diathesis model

A stress-diathesis model may provide the best opportunity for understanding the development of anxiety disorders. Clearly, individuals differ in their vulnerability to these disorders, which may reflect the operation of both inherited mechanisms and the effects of early experience. However, additional environmental stressors are required to translate this vulnerability into illness. The individual's coping style and behavioural responses then help in shaping the longer term outlook for the disorder. PTSD is, perhaps, the anxiety disorder that is explained most fully by the stress-diathesis model. Clearly the magnitude and nature of the trauma are important, but by no means all exposed individuals develop longer term problems, so individual differences must play a part as well. There is evidence that differences in coping strategies, together with opportunities for the individual to make sense for themselves of the experience, are influential in determining whether the individual goes on to develop problems (Mikhliner and Solomon 1988).

Review exercise

Write a short paragraph about each of the following terms, explaining what they mean in relation to anxiety disorders:

- preparedness
- two-process theory
- conditioned response
- vulnerability schema
- the stress-diathesis model

Summary

Explanations for the causes of anxiety disorders range from the idea that anxiety results from unresolved subconscious conflicts, to the view that anxiety is caused by disturbed function of particular neurotransmitter systems. Psychologists, in particular, have provided a number of valuable insights into the development of these disorders, implicating inappropriate learning and dysfunctional cognitive mechanisms. Psychological approaches have also resulted in the development of an extensive range of effective treatments.

Further reading

Rachman, S. (1998) *Anxiety*, Hove: Psychology Press. A concise up-to-date review of theories about and research into anxiety disorders, with a strong behavioural slant.

Eating disorders

Introduction

In this chapter, we use the term *eating disorder* to refer to the conditions of anorexia nervosa and bulimia nervosa. In both disorders there are concerns about food, body shape and weight. Until recently both were largely confined to societies in the western world, in which thinness for women is considered attractive. They appear with greater frequency in all-female environments, such as boarding schools and in particular occupational groups, such as models and dancers, in which thinness is valued. However, there is now evidence that the eating disorders are becoming more common in developing countries. The reason for this is not known, but it may be related to the establishment of 'western' ideas of attractiveness in these cultures.

Overwhelmingly, both anorexia and bulimia nervosa are disorders affecting females, although about one in twenty sufferers is male. Anorexia nervosa is more likely to occur in the higher socio-economic groups. In the United Kingdom up to 1 per cent of adolescent girls suffer from anorexia nervosa. Bulimia nervosa is more common, affecting up to 2 per cent of women between the ages of sixteen and thirty-five. Both disorders seem to be becoming more widespread.

In many respects, anorexia and bulimia nervosa represent the 'tip of the iceberg'. There are many young people who, while not showing all of the signs of these illnesses, nonetheless have difficulties with eating and body shape. These people are encountered in large numbers in health clubs, or in slimming and exercise classes.

Anorexia nervosa

Clinical features

Anorexia nervosa has three central features. The first is an extreme concern about body shape, weight and thinness. Many people today have such concerns, but in anorexia nervosa these are very much more pronounced than normal. Patients could even be described as having a morbid fear of being fat. The second major feature is the active pursuit and maintenance of a low body weight. This is achieved by a variety of means, including dieting, vomiting or the use of laxatives, or through excessive exercise. The third feature of anorexia is the absence of menstrual periods (known as *amenorrhoea*), which is directly related to low body weight and which indicates a significant disturbance of hormonal status.

Onset

Anorexia nervosa usually develops over a period of time, often after a period of dieting. Many sufferers are overweight when dieting first begins. The onset of symptoms very often follows a period of personal stress or difficulty, particularly where self-esteem is threatened. Patients may recall, for example, starting to diet after being bullied at school because of their weight, or following the ending of a relationship with a boyfriend.

Effects on relationships with family and friends

Typically sufferers have symptoms for many months before help is sought. By this time, eating patterns may have become markedly abnormal, leading to repeated angry conflicts with relatives over diet, weight and lifestyle. Relationships with friends can be disrupted and patients often become progressively more distanced and isolated from their peer group.

Concern with food

Many patients derive satisfaction from exercising precise control over their diet, body weight and appearance. For some, eating itself becomes a source of anxiety. Others can eat normally but then induce vomiting. Some patients restrict their food intake quite dramatically, before 'bingeing' on excessive quantities of food. Many sufferers think about food almost all the time and this may contribute to difficulties with concentration and may affect school performance. Some patients take great care in preparing elaborate meals for others, yet refuse to eat any of the food themselves.

Personality traits

It is often reported that people with anorexia nervosa have characteristic personalities. They tend to be quiet, unassertive, anxious and sexually inexperienced. Frequently they are ambitious and achievement-orientated, but often show low self-esteem. However, these characteristics may reflect the psychological effects of the condition, rather than any previous personality. Patients with established anorexia are frequently quite miserable, appearing only to gain a grim satisfaction from controlling their food intake. Indeed many would be regarded as having a depressive illness.

Physical effects

In addition to the psychological and behavioural changes, there are also characteristic bodily changes resulting from chronic starvation. Patients become emaciated, due to the depletion of subcutaneous fat. They often have **lanugo**, a fine downy hair that grows on the arms, back and face. Blood pressure is low and, in the later stages, swelling, or oedema, of the ankles can occur as a result of an accumulation of fluid. Chronic starvation has a number of important effects on hormone levels, which can, in turn, bring about other problems, such as amenorrhoea or abnormalities in bone structure, for example.

Treatment

Treatment approaches depend, to a large extent, on the severity of the illness. Many individuals will respond to individual or group *psychotherapy*, ideally adopting a cognitive-behavioural approach. Some patients will require admission to hospital, either to a day unit or occasionally as an in-patient.

A fundamental principle of treatment is that efforts should be made to develop an alliance with the patient, in which the development of coping techniques and a return to more normal eating patterns are encouraged. There is no good evidence that the adoption of a rigidly behavioural approach, with the removal of privileges on admission and their progressive restoration as weight is regained, confers any additional benefits. It is relatively easy in the in-patient setting to restore weight to normal levels, but helping the patient to acquire the coping skills necessary to function normally outside hospital can be much more of a challenge. Perhaps because of the disruption to family life associated with severe anorexia, some patients and their families benefit from involvement in regular meetings with a professional trained in family therapy.

Prognosis

For many patients, the prospects for improvement are good, but for about one in four the disorder may lead to lifelong difficulties. Some patients eventually die from the disease, by suicide or starvation. A poorer longer term outcome is predicted by a longer duration of illness, greater severity and later age at onset. Where menstrual abnormalities are present for sustained periods, or where onset is prior to puberty, there may be lasting impairments in menstrual function and fertility. A substantial proportion of people with anorexia go on to develop bulimia nervosa.

Case study 1: Anorexia nervosa

Katie is seventeen years old and has been in treatment for anorexia for the past three years.

Her problems seemed to begin at about the time that her family moved home, when she was twelve years old. Katie found the move very unsettling, particularly as she had to change from a small school where she was happy and had many friends, to a large school in her new town.

Katie's parents are affluent and successful. Her father works for a large company as a manager, while her mother, who used to be a model, works hard in the gym to maintain her appearance. Katie has always been envious of her older sister, as she is both clever and attractive, and has always been able to make friends easily.

Katie recalls that her problems developed after a period of dieting. Initially she had felt overweight and unattractive, and had gained satisfaction from dieting. However, over a period of months, she began to diet more seriously. She stopped eating at school, but would tell her mother that she had eaten a full lunch. She seemed to lose contact with her friends and began to go for a run every lunchtime, instead of socialising with the other children.

For a short while, Katie tried to reduce her weight by vomiting or by taking laxatives, but she stopped doing this because of how ill it made her feel. Eventually she found that she could control her weight quite well, just by exercise and diet alone.

For the first few years, she had felt quite happy about her weight, but – particularly at times of stress, such as exam time or following arguments at school – she tended to 'lose control' and to step up her dieting and exercise regime. It was during one of these times that her parents had finally confronted her about her weight and had insisted that she see the doctor.

She was referred to a psychiatrist who specialised in eating disorders. After a long discussion, she was introduced to the therapist whom she would see regularly for the next few years.

By this time, Katie agreed that she had a problem, as she felt miserable most of the time and often physically unwell too. Although she regularly felt weak and was very sensitive to the cold, she was proud of the fact that she could easily run twelve miles and could do over a hundred press-ups.

Her therapist adopted a cognitive-behavioural approach to her treatment. Together, they identified the goals that Katie would work towards, and also the thoughts and feelings that seemed to be perpetuating Katie's problems. A major problem was self-esteem, in that Katie was prone to self-criticism. She also compared herself unfavourably with her sister and with other girls of her own age. Together, the therapist and Katie agreed that the only activities from which Katie gained any satisfaction were dieting and exercise. A major task was to identify activities that Katie could take up and gain satisfaction from, but which would not further reinforce her eating disorder. Painting and reading were chosen.

For the first few months, things seemed to go well. Katie began to eat more and she reduced her dependence on running. For no obvious reason, there was then a major set-back, in which her weight plummeted and she began to diet and exercise to a more severe degree than ever before. Admission to hospital was discussed, but neither Katie nor her family were in favour, so she carried on at home. A few weeks later, things had improved and she seemed once again to be making progress.

This pattern of improvement followed by set-back continued for the next few months. After a while, family sessions were arranged, so that Katie's parents could discuss their concerns with both Katie and the therapist. At first her parents were unenthusiastic, saying that it was not them that had the problem. However, having attended a few sessions, they agreed that arguments they had been having with Katie over her eating seemed to be less of a problem.

Katie now sees her therapist fortnightly. Her weight is not yet normal and her periods are still irregular, but she is able to eat with her family and she usually eats some lunch every day at school. She now sees that dieting and exercise were, for her, ways of dealing with feelings of unhappiness and inferiority. She has tried to learn some new ways of dealing with the stresses of attending school. She still likes to run but has agreed to ration this to only twelve miles per week. She appreciates that she may remain vulnerable for quite some time to problems with her weight, but she is now making plans to take her A-levels and to attend university.

Using the following headings, describe the problems seen in anorexia nervosa:

- concern with food
- pursuit of low body weight
- effects on the body
- consequences for relationships with others

Progress exercise

Bulimia nervosa

Clinical features

Like people with anorexia nervosa, those with bulimia nervosa tend to be over-concerned about their weight and they may attempt to control this by dieting, exercise, vomiting and laxative abuse. Unlike anorexia nervosa, bulimia nervosa is associated with a near-normal body weight, but episodes of binge-eating followed by vomiting or purging are typical features. The binges, during which extraordinary quantities of food may be eaten, can occur on a daily basis. Symptoms of anxiety and depression are common, and a substantial minority of individuals with bulimia nervosa also abuse drugs or alcohol.

Bulimia nervosa and anorexia nervosa appear to be closely related disorders. The two share many features and it is common for people to move from one disorder to the other, particularly from anorexia nervosa to bulimia. Many patients with bulimia nervosa seem to begin with an illness resembling anorexia nervosa, but over time the concern with body shape becomes less prominent and weight returns to normal. However, the patient is left with the habits of bingeing and vomiting.

Treatment

The preferred treatment is a form of psychotherapy, using a cognitive-behavioural approach. Using these procedures, many patients appear to be able to increase the degree of control that they exercise over their bingeing and to normalise their diet. Drugs from one particular class of antidepressants, the SSRIs, appear to be useful in reducing the frequency of bingeing, even if symptoms of depression are absent. When treatments are compared, a consistent finding is that behavioural procedures lead to better outcomes than drug treatments, although there is some evidence that individuals gain additional benefit from the combination of the two treatments (Agras *et al.* 1992).

Prognosis

Little is known about the longer term course and outcome of bulimia nervosa, as there have been few longitudinal studies. The available evidence suggests that many patients are able to normalise their eating habits, with about two-thirds no longer fulfilling the diagnostic criteria after one year (Hsu 1990). Research indicates that further relapses are quite likely irrespective of treatment, although these appear less likely following behavioural interventions than after withdrawal from medication (Fairburn *et al.* 1991).

Case study 2: Bulimia nervosa

Amanda is a thirty-year-old office manager. She visited her family doctor as she was worried that her tendency to binge and vomit was getting out of control.

She had been concerned about her weight for many years and had tended to follow one diet with another. She thought of herself as being about half-a-stone overweight, but her friends would always tell her that she had the ideal figure for her height. Despite dieting, her weight never seemed to vary by very much. She used to go to the staff gymnasium every week, but felt self-conscious and less attractive than the other women there.

For at least ten years, she had had periods during which she would binge and vomit. At times she would eat enormous amounts of food, buying chocolate bars and sandwiches on her way to and from work. Often she would get up in the middle of the night to eat food from the freezer, which she would do hurriedly and without any apparent enjoyment. Afterwards she would feel embarrassed and be unable to understand why she had eaten so much. Feeling ashamed, she would then make herself vomit, as she had found that if she did not, she would be unhappy for hours afterwards. After vomiting, she usually felt 'normal' once more and she would often tell herself that she wasn't going to vomit or binge again.

For the past eight weeks she had begun to worry that her bingeing and vomiting was getting out of control. There were problems at work and she had felt anxious over her future and the possibility that she might have to move jobs. She remembered leaving the office at lunchtime to buy food, then vomiting on her return. She had begun to binge not only at lunchtime, but in the mornings and at night as well. A few times she had become concerned that her husband suspected she was vomiting and she had found herself making feeble excuses to put him off.

She had hoped that this episode, like all the others, would improve after a few weeks. Unfortunately she seemed to be getting worse, rather than better. She had noticed that she was getting anxious about the prospect of further bingeing, or about her husband learning of her problem, and this anxiety was affecting her concentration at work.

Amanda was referred to her local eating disorders service,

which was run by a team of psychiatrists and psychologists. A therapist showed her some simple behavioural techniques that she could use to gain back some control over the problem. She began to keep a diary, setting out her feelings through the day, together with her food intake and bingeing. It became clear that her binges tended to be preceded by feelings of anxiety, low mood, poor self-confidence and inferiority. Amanda and her therapist worked to develop ways of dealing more constructively with these feelings, rather than resorting to bingeing.

Later on in therapy, Amanda realised that she could exercise some control of her binges, once these had started, rather than feel that there was nothing that she could do once she had begun to binge. Although Amanda was not depressed, she was prescribed an SSRI antidepressant, as these drugs can be effective in reducing the frequency of binges, even in bulimic patients who are not depressed.

After two months, Amanda felt more aware than previously about her tendency to binge and she now had resources available to her by which she could exercise some control. Amanda was advised to continue medication for at least six months. Although she was aware that there may be a recurrence of bingeing in the future, she was now more optimistic that she would be able to deal with this.

Summative exercise

In terms of (a) clinical features, (b) treatment and (c) prognosis, identify *one* similarity and *one* difference between anorexia and bulimia.

Summary

We have reviewed the clinical characteristics, treatment and outcome of the two major forms of eating disorder. Each is marked by a preoccupation with food intake and body shape. In anorexia pronounced weight loss is the prominent feature, whereas in bulimia control of normal body weight is maintained despite episodes of binge-eating and purging. There is a preference to treat individuals with either disorder as out-patients, using cognitively oriented psychological therapies. In-patient care is sometimes appropriate for people with anorexia.

er reading

Hsu, L.K. (1990) *Eating Disorders*, New York: Guilford. A detailed introduction to anorexia, bulimia and other eating disorders.

10

Vulnerability and perpetuating factors in eating disorders

Introduction
Vulnerability factors
Perpetuating factors
Summary

Introduction

As with many psychological disorders, the development of anorexia and bulimia reflect the interaction of physical, psychological and social influences. Compared with the affective disorders, anxiety and schizophrenia, there has been relatively little aetiological research in this area, and it is thus more appropriate to consider factors which may influence *vulnerability* to eating disorders, rather than those that directly cause them. It is also worthwhile considering how eating disorders, once established, are *perpetuated*.

Vulnerability factors

Genetic vulnerability

There is evidence of a genetic vulnerability to anorexia nervosa. The risk of anorexia is greater in those who have a family history of the disorder. For example, about 10 per cent of the sisters of patients with anorexia nervosa themselves go on to develop the condition, compared with only 1 to 2 per cent of the general population (Theander 1970). This increase may, of course, be the consequence of a shared family environment, rather than the result of purely genetic factors. However, studies of identical (MZ) and non-identical (DZ) twins further support the suggestion of genetic vulnerability, with much higher rates of concordance in MZ than DZ twins (Holland *et al.* 1984). (See Chapter 3 for a fuller explanation of the significance of MZ:DZ concordance rates.) There is also evidence for a genetic vulnerability to bulimia nervosa (Sullivan *et al.* 1998).

The feminist perspective

A number of writers (e.g. Bemis 1978) have suggested that eating disorders result from attempts by adolescent females to conform to a stereotyped and unrealistic female form, as frequently portrayed in the media. There is strong, yet circumstantial, evidence that would support this proposal. First, as we already mentioned, anorexia nervosa appears to be much more common among women from particular occupational groups in which body shape is important and thinness valued. Second, the disorder is much more common in western societies, in which thinness in women is regarded as desirable.

The psychoanalytic perspective

The psychoanalyst, Bruch (1974), was among the first to suggest that a disturbance of body image is of central importance in the development of anorexia nervosa. She regarded people with anorexia as being engaged in a struggle, both for control and for a sense of identity. The pursuit of thinness, she proposed, was simply an extreme step in this struggle. Bruch identified two attributes of *parents* that she felt predisposed the children to anorexia. First, there was an over-concern with food. Second, the pattern of family relationships left the developing child with no sense of identity. In particular Bruch suggested that there was an abnormality in the relationship between mother and daughter, such that the child grew up feeling that her needs were of secondary importance to those of her mother. As with many psychoanalytic ideas, there is a distinct lack of experimental evidence, although there is some circumstantial evidence from case reports that might be consistent with these views.

Refuge from the demands of puberty

Crisp (1977) proposed that the changes in body shape and menstruation associated with anorexia may be a form of regression to childhood and thus an escape from the emotional problems of adolescence. This would suggest that anorexic individuals were not ready for the demands of adolescence. The observation that many anorexic people, prior to the development of their illness, are unassertive and lacking in self-esteem would be consistent with this view. It is also often said that sufferers with anorexia nervosa are immature in terms of psychosexual development. However, this issue has been examined by Beaumont, Abram *et al.* (1981), who found that while a substantial proportion of female anorexic patients were anxious or ill-informed about sexual matters, the majority of patients were normal or near-normal. Furthermore, and as with psychoanalytic explanations, these approaches tend to ignore the fact that a proportion of sufferers are male. Finally, the enduring nature of bulimia and especially anorexia nervosa suggests the influence of less short-lived factors than the journey through puberty.

Relationship with sexual abuse

Over recent years evidence has accumulated that many individuals with bulimia nervosa have experienced sexual abuse during childhood. This observation led to speculation that sexual abuse in childhood might be important in the development of bulimia, perhaps by lowering self-esteem. This issue has been examined in some detail. However, the available evidence shows that greater levels of sexual abuse in childhood are found in patients with psychiatric disorders of all types, rather than just those with bulimia nervosa. Therefore it seems that while the experience of sexual abuse in childhood may serve to increase vulnerability to psychiatric disorder, it does so in a non-specific way.

Family interactions

There has been a great deal of speculation about the possible effects that abnormalities in relationships within the family may have on the development of eating disorders. Minuchin, for example, has characterised the families of anorexic people as being dysfunctional in a number of ways (Minuchin *et al.* 1978). Family members, he suggests, tend to be over-involved in each other's lives and to respond inflexibly when confronted by novel situations. They are also described as lacking the skills needed to resolve the conflict. Therefore they tend to *suppress* the conflict, rather than seek solutions to their family disputes. One can imagine a family in which these characteristics were dominant to be seething with discontent, yet with no hope for easy resolution of difficulties. Minuchin identified these conditions as being ideal for the development of anorexia nervosa in a younger female member. According to this view, the illness of the patient serves to prevent overt conflict within the family by diverting attention away from the conflict and on to themselves. Thus there can be little hope for improvement, as this would lead to increased family conflict and therefore would be resisted by other family members.

Theories of this sort have at least four major shortcomings. First, it is not specified why the person develops anorexia nervosa, rather than any other medical illness, which might equally act to reduce conflict. Second, it is unclear why this should affect girls so much more often than boys. Third, families with these characteristics have probably existed throughout history, yet anorexia nervosa is a disease of modern western societies. Finally, it has yet to be demonstrated that these characteristics are found more commonly in the families of anorexia sufferers than in the general population. Even if this were the case, it may be that such abnormalities are a consequence, rather than cause, of anorexia nervosa within the family.

In the context of vulnerability to developing eating disorders, describe the insights that have been provided by writers from each of the following standpoints:

- genetic studies
- feminism
- psychoanalytic perspective
- family interactions

Try to identify the limitations of each of these proposals.

Progress exercise:

Perpetuating factors

The changes in diet and exercise that lead to weight loss in anorexia appear to be sustained by a range of psychological and physical mechanisms.

Socially, the disruption of relationships with family and peers may perpetuate the disorder and clearly makes restoration of a normal lifestyle more of a challenge.

In addition, the patient may value the sense of control that comes with strict dieting. Initially at least there may be approval from others about weight loss and body shape. Thus a form of conditioning may come to operate, in which weight loss is reinforced by the dual mechanisms of self- and peer-approval. Why then does the weight loss continue past normal levels of thinness? If one sees the attention gained through approval as the reinforcer, rather than the approval itself, then conditioning could explain the continued weight loss. Becoming more and more ill would continue to attract attention and thereby maintain the reinforcement.

Cognitive explanations of eating disorders focus on the central idea of an over-valued and unhealthy concern with the importance of body weight and shape. These *core* beliefs also determine and perpetuate many other aspects of the full clinical picture. Thus self-worth comes to be measured in terms of how effectively control of body weight and shape is achieved. The person comes to think of fatness as extremely undesirable, whereas being slim is attractive and desirable.

Self-control, achieved through constant weighing, calorie-counting, purging and so on, also comes to assume central importance in the quest for ideal body physique. To some extent these beliefs are no more than exaggerations of the views common to many people. It is the sense of personal significance, coupled with the dysfunctional reasoning and behaviour, that differentiates someone with an eating disorder from the person who simply wishes to keep in shape.

Although this argument explains the maintenance of anorexia, it is less satisfactory in accounting for the enduring features of bulimia. For example, if control of body weight was the central issue, we might expect that fear of weight gain would simply lead to constant dieting and that restoration of normal weight might be followed by even more severe dieting. In fact neither of these things happens in bulimia. Sufferers with bulimia are not very good at sticking to diets in the first place and having transgressed, they may then go to the other extreme and overeat.

Physical factors may have the effect of perpetuating anorexia nervosa, once it has become established. Starvation, even in otherwise healthy people, is known to lead to increased concern with food and to reduced interest in the outside world. Prolonged food deprivation also affects the working of the digestive system so that eating even small quantities of food results in an exaggerated sense of fullness: something which would, of course, perpetuate the disorder.

Disturbances in neurotransmitter function have also been examined in relation to the maintenance of eating disorders. The evidence is strongest for bulimia nervosa. The neurotransmitter 5-HT (serotonin) is involved in the regulation of appetite and it has been suggested that bingeing may reflect dysfunction of these systems. This proposal is supported by the observation that SSRI drugs, which are known to influence brain serotonin systems, can lead to dramatic reductions in the frequency of bingeing.

Summary

Both anorexia nervosa and bulimia nervosa are often explained solely on the basis of psychological, social or family factors, but, as we have seen, somatogenic influences may be equally important and a full understanding will involve the integration of all of these approaches. Longitudinal research on eating disorders is lacking and there is a real need for comprehensive evaluations of the effects of different interventions on long-term outcome.

Re-read the case studies of Katie and Amanda from the previous chapter, and identify the key perpetuating factors that appear to influence the course of their eating disorders.

Review exercise

Further reading

Hsu, L.K. (1990) *Eating Disorders*, New York: Guilford. A detailed introduction to anorexia, bulimia and other eating disorders.

Garner, D.M. and Garfinkel, P.E. (1985) *Handbook of Psychotherapy for Anorexia Nervosa and Bulimia Nervosa*, New York: Guilford. Therapeutic strategies for managing anorexic and bulimic clients.

11

Criticisms of psychopathology

Introduction

Modern psychopathology tries to offer a coherent conceptual framework that best fits current knowledge and understanding of mental disorders. It has shown itself willing to adapt in light of new evidence about causation or treatment, to embrace new methodologies and to abandon cherished but outmoded concepts. This is an ongoing process and further change is inevitable as new research findings are published.

In previous chapters we have identified issues or ideas which have been the focus for heated debate within psychopathology. Generally we have not pursued these if, on balance, their impact has only been short-lived or they have not attracted widespread interest. (Bateson's double-bind theory, discussed in Chapter 4, might be a case in point.)

However, in this chapter, we identify some of the more enduring criticisms of psychopathology and try to evaluate their present status. It is no coincidence that many of these concerns relate particularly to schizophrenia and its treatment. As you will now know, this disorder remains one of the most disabling, severe and perplexing of mental illnesses, accounting for more involuntary hospital admissions than any other. In the minds of some observers at least, it has almost come to symbolise mental illness in general; hence the disproportionate attention that it seems to attract. As you read this material, remember that there is no coherent *anti-psychopathology* viewpoint. Rather there are a range of ideas whose only common thread is one of dissatisfaction with the status quo.

Mental illness does not exist

The most extreme criticism of psychopathology is that mental illnesses do not, in fact, exist. In this view, scientific psychopathology simply provides a framework, sanctioned by the establishment or the state, to deal with people who do not fit the conventional view of normal human behaviour. In other words, mental hospitals serve as repositories for undesirable antisocial non-conforming individuals, with psychiatrists as gatekeepers.

Szasz's 'myth of mental illness'

The principal and most persistent proponent of this viewpoint is Szasz. He has argued that as most patients with mental illness do not have a brain disease that might cause their symptoms, such as epilepsy or a tumour, they cannot be described as having an 'illness'. He regards the term 'mental illness' as a contradiction in terms, principally because the mind, as distinct from the brain, is a hypothetical construct rather than a physical organ, and as such cannot be diseased (Szasz 1960). Szasz regards the mentally ill as having 'problems of living', and suggests that they might be better off consulting counsellors or psychotherapists rather than psychiatrists (Szasz 1985). According to him, the principal role in society of psychiatrists is to authorise and make respectable the process of involuntary hospitalisation.

A key element of Szasz's argument is that of personal responsibility. (In this respect he has much in common with supporters of the humanist approach, who also emphasise the responsibility of the individual.) He appears to believe that all people, including those with mental health problems, should retain responsibility for themselves and their lives. Psychologists and psychiatrists, as outsiders, have no right to interfere unless an individual represents a threat to other people. Szasz is not against treatment *per se*, as long as the individual *chooses* it. This idea is reiterated in his views about suicide, which is a major cause of death for people with a severe mental illness. He has suggested, for example, that if someone wishes to kill themselves, then that is their business and no one else has the right to intervene.

Comment

What should we make of these ideas? Clearly mental health services *are* sanctioned by the state and some patients are admitted and treated *against their will* – in Britain, under the terms of the Mental Health Act. In our view, however, mental health services exist not to punish or restrict the freedom of patients or service users, but because *mental illness exists.*

This point was rather clearly illustrated by a series of events that unfolded in Italy in the late 1970s and early 1980s following the rise to prominence and election of members of the group **Psichiatrica Democratica**. One of their election pledges was to close all large mental hospitals and to set up smaller units in general hospitals instead. An act was hastily passed introducing this law, although provision of alternative, community-based facilities was decidedly patchy. The upshot was that general hospitals rapidly became overwhelmed with former asylum patients seeking treatment. It has been estimated that the use of antipsychotic drugs actually *increased* for these acutely ill patients, some of whom, ironically, found accommodation in the very hospitals that had been closed, only to be reopened as 'community facilities' (Jones and Poletti 1986).

Another of Szasz's concerns is the use of treatments against a person's will; something which certainly does happen to a proportion of people in mental hospitals. However we might usefully ask what happens to these individuals when they are discharged from hospital: do they, for example, throw away their medicines vowing never to take them again? In a recent study, we interviewed thirty-five out-patients with schizophrenia, asking about their attitudes to medication. Every one of our patients reported that they had stopped taking their medication at some time, either because they felt better or because of unpleasant side-effects. Yet all but one had *started* again, usually to stave off the reappearance of psychotic symptoms. Thus, despite their unpleasant side-effects, it would seem that patients usually come to recognise the value of medication in reducing the likelihood of relapse. In the United Kingdom at present, about nine out of ten individuals with a diagnosis of schizophrenia will not be in hospital, yet most will continue to take medication, despite there being no formal mechanisms to compel them.

Thus our overall impression of Szasz's viewpoint is that it simply doesn't fit the facts. First, while people with mental illnesses should, in general, be held responsible for their actions, mental illness can *and sometimes does* impair thinking to the extent that people cannot be considered responsible. (Indeed we view it as a measure of a civilised society that its legal system can make allowances in this way.) Second, the Italian experience has shown that mental illness does not disappear when mental hospitals are closed. Third, it is also of interest to us to note that, in the long run, patients often gain considerable *insight* into the waxing and waning nature of their illness. They learn the 'danger signs' and understand when to take new medication, to increase current dose, or perhaps to seek extra support.

Despite these criticisms, Szasz's perspective has had one lasting and beneficial effect. By promoting his views so strongly, he has forced orthodox psychopathology to strive even harder to fully understand the nature of mental illnesses and to counter his arguments.

Mental illness as a deliberate response

Early psycho-social models

A second relatively enduring criticism is that mental illnesses are rational responses to intolerable social circumstances. We outlined some these ideas in Chapter 4, pointing out that empirical support for each was weak. Nevertheless, in the early 1960s, these ideas were taken up by a group of psychiatrists, headed by Laing, who had become dissatisfied with orthodox psychiatry. The so-called *antipsychiatry* group looked for evidence of the harmful effects of family life, using case studies. Several cases were described to illustrate the 'rational' withdrawal into schizophrenia made by individuals faced with intolerable domestic circumstances. Since mental illnesses were seen as semi-voluntary states, treatments were developed to focus on guiding the individual through the experience, rather than on changing behaviour with drugs. These alternative treatments included counselling and *encounter group* work, and particularly family therapy. *Therapeutic communities* were set up, in the United Kingdom most notably Kingsley Hall, as alternatives to mental hospitals.

Comment

We mentioned earlier the lack of supportive evidence for the ideas of Bateson, Lidz and colleagues. Laing and Esterson's work (1970) has additionally been criticised for use of the case-study method. Although clinical cases are presented to support their arguments, they do not include 'control' cases; that is people with similar family backgrounds who do not have a mental illness. This means that it is impossible to say whether or not particular family dynamics are unique to the households in which one member goes on to develop a mental illness. Subsequent research by Henry (1973) and Hirsch (1979) has shown that these problems in family relationships and communication are, in fact, relatively common features of family life in general. More recent evidence from EE research (see Chapter 4) has suggested that far from precipitating mental illness, the family can act as a buffer against the stresses of everyday life, and so may delay or prevent it. Thus, on balance, criticisms of the family seem unwarranted.

Proper evaluation of the effectiveness of the original therapeutic communities is also difficult, because the criteria used to recruit people were vague. It has been suggested that participants were an atypical sample, being for the most part young, articulate, intelligent and only moderately disturbed. Also there is no follow-up evidence that would allow us to judge how the patients fared in the longer term.

Our final comment relates to the central idea of supporters of this approach; namely that severe mental illness is, in some sense, *a matter of choice*. The available evidence and our own clinical experience lead us to quite the opposite conclusion. Patients with psychotic disorders often describe their symptoms as if they are the passive recipients of them. They often find their experiences frightening and they will sometimes go to extraordinary lengths to try to get rid of them. Depressed patients often describe their state of mind in terms that indicate the sense of being a victim of circumstance. Many patients with anxiety disorders seek help, believing they have a physical (rather than a psychological) disorder. None of these observations fit in well with a model in which illness is an option that individuals may take or leave.

Disease, syndrome or symptoms?

The right level of enquiry

This issue is as much a matter of debate as a criticism. Since the term 'disease' defines an illness with specific symptoms, a known cause and usually a clear-cut outcome, many people consider it is an unsuitable term for mental illnesses. In psychopathology, we generally think of mental disorders as *syndromes*. (A syndrome is just a cluster of symptoms that tend to occur together, where there need be no understanding of cause, nor common outcome.) However critics of this viewpoint argue that this level of enquiry is inappropriate. Although they may accept many of the basic ideas in conventional psychopathology, they argue that there is no justification for sticking with terms such as schizophrenia or bipolar disorder, which they regard as imprecise and ill-defined. Other critics seem less concerned with the diagnostic name. Nevertheless they still advocate a re-direction of attention towards individual symptoms.

Bentall (1990) has consistently criticised the use of the term schizophrenia, arguing that it lacks reliability, is without construct or predictive validity, has no defining symptoms (i.e. symptoms unique to it) and no common underlying aetiology. In his view these problems render schizophrenia a rather meaningless diagnostic label, which should be abandoned in the pursuit of a better understanding of psychotic symptoms.

Others have suggested that, while the concept of schizophrenia may be worth retaining, it still makes more sense to focus research efforts on individual symptoms. These may have a common aetiology, even when they appear in different illnesses. For example, in Chapter 4 we described Frith's theory about the origin of certain alien control symptoms (delusions of control, passivity phenomena) found in schizophrenia. However he has suggested that his theory may also explain the occurrence of similar symptoms in other disorders, such as the drug-induced disorder **amphetamine psychosis**, Huntington's Disease (a genetically determined neurological disorder) and certain rare but intriguing neurological conditions such as alien-hand syndrome (in which patients 'disown' the actions of one of their hands).

Comment

Should we therefore follow Bentall's advice and abandon forthwith the use of syndromal names like schizophrenia and anxiety? We think not, or at least not yet. Consider for a moment some of the findings of the WHO pilot study in schizophrenia, which is widely regarded as a milestone in sound epidemiological research. (See our review in Chapter 13.) The research showed that, at the time of diagnosis, 74 per cent of patients were experiencing some form of hallucination, 65 per cent had delusions and over 90 per cent showed evidence of disordered thinking. We think that this is strong evidence in support of the argument that schizophrenia truly is a **syndromal disorder**, rather than a collection of unrelated symptoms.

This view is reinforced by studies that have employed **factor analysis** (a type of statistical analysis) to show how the individual symptoms of schizophrenia tend to cluster together, rather than appear in isolation. Liddle's three factor model of schizophrenia (1987), described in Chapter 3, would be one example of this research approach.

Categorical versus dimensional classification

A mental health continuum?

As we mentioned in Chapter 2, the ICD and DSM diagnostic systems involve categories of mental disorder. Each has some notional threshold, based on symptom intensity and duration, coping and so on. A patient fulfilling these criteria is deemed to *have* the disorder. Sometimes an individual may be so ill at the time of diagnosis that this arrangement works well. However there will also be some people whose mental state wavers around the threshold. (If you are wondering why this is an issue, remember that a decision about whether or not a person has a mental illness may affect whether they can be treated against their will, or may have far-reaching legal implications.)

The fact that symptoms lie on a continuum of severity is especially well-illustrated by recent investigations into their prevalence amongst members of the general population. One symptom that has come under particular scrutiny is the experience of auditory hallucinations. (Remember that several forms of this symptom are regarded as evidence of schizophrenia in DSM and ICD.) Romme and Escher (1989) identified several hundred people, many with no prior history of mental illness, who claimed to 'hear voices'. Further investigation has confirmed that a significant proportion of the non-clinical population (estimated in Johns 1998 to be in the region of 5 per cent) do indeed have this experience on a reasonably regular basis. The same seems also to be true for delusions (Peters *et al.* 1998), depression and anxiety (Brown and Harris 1978).

This evidence has been seized upon by people eager to criticise psychopathology. A number of mental health pressure groups have recently argued that this research shows that it is 'normal' to hear voices and therefore that auditory hallucinations should not be regarded as symptoms of mental illness. We do not share this view, since the evidence indicates that, statistically at least, it is still quite unusual to do so. However, the fact that even a proportion of otherwise mentally well people sometimes experience these symptoms is of interest. This research tends to support the dimensional approach, because it suggests that psychiatric symptoms are *a matter of degree*, rather than being qualitatively distinct defining characteristics.

Too much or too little science?

A final area of concern is the relationship between psychopathology and science. In this instance at least, it seems that psychopathology cannot win. On the one hand, hard scientists in other branches of medicine argue that psychopathology lacks scientific rigour. On the other hand, counsellors, psychotherapists and sometimes patients argue that psychopathology is steadily becoming too scientific and, in the process, is losing 'the human touch'.

In writing this book, we have taken the view that psychopathology has developed to its current position largely because of its willingness to stand or fall in the light of scientific research. We admit to disagreeing (slightly!) between ourselves about how scientific psychopathology actually is, or ever can be, but we concur with Clare (1980) in rejecting outright the proposal that it should become less scientific. If one of us developed a mental illness, we would hope that any treatments we were given had been properly validated and tested. Moreover, if the initial treatment did not have the desired effect, we would expect that the clinician in question would, as a **scientist-practitioner**, consider his initial hypothesis rejected and move on to test a second hypothesis, i.e. to suggest an alternative approach to treatment.

It is often claimed that endorsement of a scientific approach in psychopathology simply reinforces the biological paradigm (Ingleby 1981). We suggest that this is also not so. Rather, it involves taking the most scientifically valid elements from *all* approaches – biological, psychological and social – and integrating this material into a coherent theory. By this process we are just as likely to find support for family therapy as for a new drug treatment. As a discipline, psychopathology may, on occasion, stray from the scientifically 'straight and narrow path'; however, our view is that it is generally pointing in the right direction and will advance further by remaining grounded in the scientific method.

Summary

We have reviewed and commented on some of the enduring criticisms of psychopathology. We suggest that for most people mental illness is neither a mythical nor a voluntary state. There is interest in research into the causes of individual symptoms, although the syndrome level continues to be the preferred way of thinking about mental illness. We are concerned that, in adopting category-based diagnostic systems like DSM and ICD, conventional psychopathology is ignoring the apparently continuous nature of some symptoms. The further development of psychopathology will depend on its continued willingness to adapt in the light of new scientific findings.

Write short notes on the pros and cons of the following criticisms of psychopathology:

- mental illness is a myth
- mental illness is a deliberate response
- symptoms rather than syndromes
- categorical versus dimensional approaches

As an additional exercise, match up the following theorists to the approaches described above:

Szasz, Laing, Bentall, Romme

Further reading

Clare, A. (1980) *Psychiatry in Dissent*, 2nd edn, London: Tavistock. A classic, if somewhat dated, personal perspective on psychopathology. The author reviews the literature and dispels several myths and misunderstandings about theory and research.

Davison, G.C. and Neale, J.M. (1998) *Abnormal Psychology*, 7th edn, New York: Wiley.

12

The future of psychopathology

Introduction

Despite its colourful history, psychopathology is only now beginning to mature as a discipline in its own right. It straddles psychiatry, clinical psychology, neurology and the neurosciences in general. Its rapid growth makes it difficult to predict developments, even in the near future. We realise that in concluding our book with an exercise in crystal-ball gazing, we will probably be obliged to eat (at least some of) our words in due course! However we think that psychopathology does have an exciting future and in the following sections we map out, in no particular order, some of the issues that we expect will shape its development in the coming years.

Unravelling brain–behaviour interactions

From links with neuroscience we are learning about the intricacies of brain biochemistry (neurotransmitter function, the action of hormones and so on) and how these chemicals can influence mood and behaviour. However it seems that many factors influence brain biochemistry in turn. Predictably these include genetic factors, nutrition, brain damage and exposure to drugs or toxins. Less predictably factors such as age, stress, bereavement, personality, and even learning and memory appear be involved. In this way they may ultimately affect mood and behaviour too. The relationship between brain and behaviour is clearly two-way.

We agree with Paykel and Hollyman (1984) who argued that there should be no artificial divide between the effects of somatic and psychological factors on the brain mechanisms that mediate mood and behaviour. One person may become depressed because of an inherited predisposition to underactivity of serotonin neurotransmission, while another may develop the same symptoms for quite different reasons, as a consequence of prolonged exposure to stress, for example, or following the birth of a child. The picture that is now emerging of the relationship between brain function and behaviour is a far more dynamic one than ever before. The current trend is to consider brain connectivity as **plastic** rather than **hard-wired**, with brain and behaviour each influencing the other.

Progress exercise

Identify (a) four physiological, and (b) four experiential factors known to influence brain function.

More eclecticism

We now have a clearer idea of how biological and psychological therapies might independently influence behaviour, albeit by different routes. This should lead to greater collaboration between supporters of the various paradigms described in Chapter 2. We have already seen specific examples of the value of eclectic or combined treatment approaches for disorders such as depression and certain forms of schizophrenia, and we would hope and expect this approach to apply to other disorders too. We are learning that many disorders may have multiple interactive causes, and this trend away from the quest for identification of a single cause for a given disorder is likely to gain momentum.

Genetic mechanisms and testing

Conservative estimates suggest that approximately one third of the 100,000 or so genes each of us inherits exerts some influence on brain structure and function. Evidence drawn from twin, adoption and high-risk studies indicates that we each inherit genes that change our risk of developing all sorts of diseases, including mental illnesses (Gottesman 1991).

There are a number of mental illnesses for which we can be confident that genetic factors are involved, but we do not know as yet how these factors predispose us to illness. Simple single-gene patterns of inheritance (as seen in Huntington's disease or **PKU**) seem not to apply, so it is assumed that multiple genes are involved. At present, however, we have little idea about just how many genes are involved, how they interact, or what they do. But as techniques in molecular genetics develop and the human genome project (the mapping of all human genes to their positions on particular chromosomes) reaches its conclusion, this situation is likely to change. It should be possible to identify with some confidence genes that are linked to particular disorders, to say what they do normally, and to understand how they influence the predisposition towards disorder. Once this is known, diagnostic tests will soon follow that permit assessment of risk. It may even be possible to assess risk in the unborn child.

New treatments

As our understanding of brain biochemistry has grown, so too has the ability of pharmacologists to develop drugs with specific actions, for example, to target particular neurotransmitter receptors. Over recent years we have seen the development of new types of medication for use in depressive illness and schizophrenia. Despite their cost, these drugs look set to replace many of the older drugs, because they are more effective and have fewer side-effects (Thomas and Lewis 1998). For each of the newer drugs now available, there are at least as many experimental substances currently under development, so the next few years look set to herald the arrival of many new and better drugs (Kerwin and Taylor 1996).

We anticipate that psychotherapies will also become more widely used in future. They may have particular value when used in combination with medication. Although cognitive-behaviour therapy has existed for over twenty years and has now been widely adopted as a treatment for depression, its application to some other psychiatric disorders is only just being assessed. Preliminary results suggest that it may be of particular use in treating panic attacks (Chambless and Gillis 1993) and specific symptoms in schizophrenia (Hodel and Brenner 1994). Other forms of psychotherapy have also recently attracted renewed interest. Inter-personal therapy (IPT), for example, seems effective in reducing the risk of further episodes of depression (Elkin *et al.* 1985), while personal therapy may be useful, in combination with medication, in improving social functioning in people recovering from schizophrenia (Hogarty *et al.* 1997).

Greater use of imaging techniques

The development of the new brain-imaging techniques is already beginning to have a major impact on our understanding of brain–behaviour relations in the context of mental illness. As new techniques become more widely established, psychopathology will reap substantial benefits.

These techniques can now be adapted to focus on the activity levels of specific neurotransmitters. PET scans have been used to measure noradrenaline function in individuals with PTSD (Bremner *et al.* 1997) and dopamine receptor activity in people with chronic schizophrenia (Okubo *et al.* 1997). Similarly, PET and *f*MRI techniques allow us to observe the functional activity of specific brain regions as the subject engages in a particular task. Very recent research has permitted identification of the parts of the brain which are involved in self-monitoring (Spence *et al.* 1997) and in memory (Murphy *et al.* 1998). In each case, use of the imaging technique offers us an insight into the change in brain activity associated with an aspect of disturbed behaviour. This is in effect *a window on the dysfunctional mind.*

Care for people with a mental illness

So far our predictions about the future of psychopathology have been consistently optimistic. However when we consider care provision for people with a mental illness, we are inclined to moderate our optimism with a dose of realism. The trend towards **community care** is one that we strongly endorse *in principle*. However, we are all too well aware of the patchy nature of care provision and the apparent void in which some people find themselves, following discharge from hospital.

The number of patients resident for long periods in psychiatric hospitals has declined year on year at least since the mid-1960s, and we hope this trend continues. But, in order for this to happen, the practice of community care needs to be reviewed, with greater resources being made available.

For some, the reality of community care is life in a bedsit with occasional visits from a community psychiatric nurse and rare trips to the hospital day-clinic. These are hardly ideal circumstances in which to recover from a mental illness. Yet with appropriate resources, community care could provide facilities that make for an altogether more effective therapeutic environment. We can envisage care packages that blend therapy sessions and practical help, that offer careers advice and retraining, that provide counselling and guidance, that run courses in stress-management and social skills, *that invite participation and discourage apathy and dependency.* Such packages are currently few and far between, despite recent illustrations of their effectiveness, even for patients with relatively severe illnesses (Muijen *et al.* 1996). We hope that, in years to come, policy-makers and politicians will come to realise that effective community care is not a cheap option, and that it can operate effectively only if it is properly planned and resourced.

Summary

Psychopathology has an exciting future. As the reciprocal relationship between brain and behaviour is unravelled, thanks in part to the wider availability of imaging technology, the stress-diathesis model of mental illness gains further support. Knowing about the precise role of genetic factors will enable us to understand how vulnerability may translate into illness. New, more precisely targeted drugs, with fewer side-effects, are beginning to replace many older ones. There is considerable interest in the wider applications of psychological treatments such as CBT or IPT. Community care provision must be properly planned and resourced, if it is to be effective.

Three research reviews

Introduction

In this chapter, we summarise three pieces of research. The first two are classic studies which we have referred to repeatedly in earlier chapters of this book. The 'International pilot study of schizophrenia' (Sartorius *et al.* 1974) is for many a milestone in epidemiological research, which explores the reliability and validity of the schizophrenia diagnosis. Elkin *et al.*'s report (1985) compares different treatment programmes for depressive illness. We have included this study because it continues to attract widespread interest, and because it was one of the first large-scale studies to show that distinct treatments can each reduce the symptoms of depression. Our third research summary is, by comparison, a much more modest project: Sanderson *et al.*'s study (1989) shows how a 'sense of being in control' affects the experience of panic. We include it because it illustrates how cognitive factors can influence emotion.

As you read these summaries, keep in mind the questions that the researchers tried to address and note how they attempted to control for the possible influences of extraneous variables. You will see that, despite their best efforts, each study can be criticised on method-ological grounds. Can you think of any ways of improving these studies to overcome their shortcomings?

Progress exercise

International pilot study of schizophrenia[1]

Background   Towards the end of the 1960s there was increasing concern about both the reliability and validity of the diagnosis of schizophrenia. This uncertainty stemmed from the results of cross-cultural studies which tended to suggest that basic ideas about what constituted mental illness were culturally specific and presented the observation that even among 'developed' countries, the rates of diag-nosis of schizophrenia and certain other mental illnesses were inconsistent. The IPSS was set up by the World Health Organisation to establish whether or not schizophrenia could be reliably diagnosed across different countries and cultures. A follow-up study (1979) permitted some measures of different aspects of validity of the diag-nosis to be examined.

METHOD   The initial sample comprised over 1,200 patients drawn from nine centres around the world. Detailed clinical assessments were undertaken using the Present State Examination (PSE), a semi-structured interview designed to cover all areas of psychopathology. Diagnoses were made by two psychiatrists working independently of one another. Of the initial sample, 811 people were identified by both clinicians as having schizophrenia.

1   N. Sartorius, R. Shapiro and A. Jablonsky (1974) 'The international pilot study of schizophrenia', *Schizophrenia Bulletin* 2: 21–35.

RESULTS The study design allows us to distinguish between results relating to reliability and those that relate to validity. For reliability the IPSS required a proportion of patients to be interviewed separately by two clinicians, who then made independent diagnoses. A total of 190 patients were assessed in this way, and inter-rater agreement was confirmed for 131 (69 per cent) of them. Although this may not seem very high, disagreement, when it occurred, usually concerned disputes about one or other category of psychosis. In only five cases was there disagreement over a psychotic or non-psychotic diagnosis.

The data also permitted consideration of three different forms of validity. *Content validity* was supported by the consistent pattern of symptoms found across the 811 consensus cases. The most prominent were lack of insight, suspiciousness, persecutory ideas, delusions and hallucinations. *Concurrent validity* was supported by the observation that almost 90 per cent of individuals diagnosed by clinicians as having schizophrenia also received the same diagnosis when the CATEGO computer diagnostic programme was used. *Predictive validity* could be assessed after publication of the two-year follow-up study, based on a subsample of 585 cases (WHO 1979). This part of the study confirmed that about one third of the sample could expect a poor outcome after two years, which was a much less optimistic picture than for other psychotic disorders. The follow-up study also highlighted a reduction in positive symptoms and the progressive emergence of negative symptoms at this stage of illness.

DISCUSSION Although we have only mentioned a small proportion of the findings from this major collaborative study, the results indicate that schizophrenia can be reliably diagnosed and that its validity can be supported using several indices. Interestingly the diagnosis and particular clinical features of schizophrenia were relatively consistent across centres, although outcome measures indicated rather better recovery rates in developing countries than in the industrialised world.

Treatment of depression collaborative research programme[2]

Background Although depression is the most frequently treated psychiatric disorder, the value of the treatments themselves, such as medication, ECT and psychotherapy, have been debated for many years. By the late 1970s, it was clear that although some patients with depression seemed to respond favourably to each of the treatments mentioned above, there was little consensus about their relative merits, nor about how the treatments should be matched to particular forms or degrees of depression. (The one exception to this was the recommendation by the 1985 consensus conference that ECT was most suited to severely ill patients who had not responded to drug therapy.) The National Institute of Mental Health in America decided to sponsor a major study, to be coordinated by Elkin and her colleagues, to look into these matters.

METHOD Researchers from six centres throughout the United States worked together to recruit 240 out-patients suffering from depressive illnesses. Patients were randomly allocated to one of four treatment conditions. One group received a course of *cognitive therapy* (CT). A second received a psychodynamically-oriented psychotherapy referred to as *inter-personal therapy* (IPT). A third group of patients were treated with the *anti-depressant medication* imipramine (IMI), while the fourth group were allocated to the placebo condition, in which they were given a dummy drug and told it might be an effective antidepressant. This was a longitudinal study, with all patients followed-up for at least sixteen weeks and some followed-up for eighteen months, enabling researchers to make repeated detailed evaluations of their condition.

RESULTS Three principle findings emerged. First, all three 'active' therapies improved patients' mood better than did placebo. Second, of the three therapies, drug treatment produced

----
2   I. Elkin, M.B. Parloff, S.W. Hadley and J.H. Autry (1985) 'NIMH treatment of depression collaborative research program', *Archives of General Psychiatry* 42: 305–16.

the fastest relief, but after sixteen weeks the other two (CT and IPT) had caught up. Finally, in the longer term patients from the CT and IPT conditions seemed less likely to experience further episodes of depression than did patients who had received the antidepressant medication.

DISCUSSION This study has contributed greatly to resolving arguments about treatment for depression. The inclusion of a placebo condition illustrates very clearly the comparative advantage resulting from all three of the active treatments. Although patients in the placebo condition improved slightly, the greater clinical improvement seen with the three active conditions shows that they bring added value to the treatment of depression.

The study suggests that for people with depressive illness of moderate severity, antidepressant medication might be the best treatment in the short term, but that some psychotherapeutic procedures may offer longer term advantages. This finding has prompted researchers to begin to evaluate the effect of *combined* treatments.

However, despite the care that went into designing this study (which included recruitment of a large sample and random allocation to treatments), disputes about the findings and their interpretation have continued for many years. First, the patients had depressive illnesses of moderate severity and therefore we cannot draw conclusions about the treatment of people with more severe illnesses. Second, the key measure in this study was the average improvement in symptoms for each treatment. However, the drop-out rate of participants from the study varied between treatments and centres, and this is likely to have biased the average recorded level of improvement. Finally, despite major efforts to standardise treatments, outcome varied *between* centres, suggesting that there were important differences in the way therapies were administered.

Notwithstanding these concerns, the NIMH study has undoubtedly influenced treatment for depression, by pointing out the advantages of a range of different treatments.

Effect of 'apparent control' on panic attacks[3]

Background   Psychologists have identified several factors or conditions that seem able to induce panic attacks. Knowledge about these parameters is of value because it might tell us something about how and why people experience panic attacks in the real world. Although the effects are most readily seen in people with a prior history of anxiety-related disorders, panic attacks may also be induced in a proportion of the non-clinical population.

One condition which reliably induces panic attacks, in both patients and those who have not previously been prone to anxiety, is the inhalation of air which has been enriched with carbon dioxide (CO_2). This was the method chosen by Sanderson and colleagues. However, in order to assess the relative contributions of cognitive factors to induced panic attacks, the researchers introduced a second variable, that of perceived control. To do this, they influenced the participants' beliefs about whether or not they could control the amount of additional CO_2 they were breathing.

METHOD   Twenty people, all meeting diagnostic criteria for panic disorder, were recruited and randomly allocated to one of two experimental conditions. All participants sat alone in a small room and were told that they would breath normal air for five minutes, then CO_2-enriched air for a further fifteen minutes. They were warned that during this period they might experience various emotions. Each participant was given a box with a light and a dial on it and were told that if the light came on, they would be able to adjust the proportion of CO_2 in the air by using the dial, if they felt it necessary. In fact, for half the participants the light was never switched on. For the remainder, the light was switched on at the beginning of the enriched CO_2 phase, although adjusting the dial actually had no effect on the CO_2 concentration.

3 W.C. Sanderson, R.M. Rapee and D.H. Barlow (1989) 'The influence of an illusion of control on panic attacks induced by inhalation of 5.5% CO_2 enriched air', *Archives of General Psychiatry* 46: 157–62.

RESULTS Although patients in both groups experienced a range of symptoms including light-headedness, breathlessness and dizziness during the enriched CO_2 phase of the study, participants who thought they were controlling the CO_2 concentration experienced far fewer panic symptoms than those in the 'no control' group. Indeed, in this group only two out of ten had a panic attack, whereas in the 'no control' group eight out of ten participants experienced an attack.

DISCUSSION The results of this study illustrate the ease with which panic attacks can be reliably induced in people with a prior history of anxiety disorder, when they are required to breath CO_2-enriched air for just a few minutes. However the most interesting finding is that beliefs about control also influence the development of panic symptoms. Individuals in the 'no control' group experienced twice as many panic symptoms as did those in the other condition.

On the other hand, it is worth remembering that the panic attacks were artificially induced and may differ, in a number of ways, from naturally-occurring panic attacks. Moreover, this study employed a very small sample and although the differences appear large, they only just reach statistical significance. Nevertheless, the study is a powerful reminder that 'sense of control' may be an important cognitive factor in determining whether or not an individual experiences a panic attack.

14

Study aids

Improving your essay writing skills

At this point in the book you have acquired the knowledge necessary to tackle the exam itself. Answering exam questions is a skill and in this chapter we hope to help you improve this skill. A common mistake that some students make is not providing the kind of evidence the examiner is looking for. Another is failing to properly answer the question, despite providing lots of information. Typically, a grade C answer is accurate and reasonably constructed, but has limited detail and commentary. To lift such an answer to an A or B grade may require no more than fuller detail, better use of material and a coherent organisation. By studying the essays below, and the comments that follow, you can learn how to turn your grade C answer into a grade A. Please note that marks given by the examiner in the practice essays should be used as a guide only and are not definitive. They represent the 'raw marks' given by an AEB examiner. That is, the marks the examiner would give to the examining board based on a total of 25 marks per question broken down into Skill A (description) and Skill B (evaluation). Tables showing this scheme are in Appendix C of Paul Humphreys' title in the series, *Exam Success in AEB Psychology*. They may not be the marks given on the examination certificate received ultimately by the student because all examining boards are required to use a common standardised system called the Uniform Mark Scale (UMS) which adjusts all raw scores to a single standard acceptable to all examining boards.

The essays are about the length a student would be able to write in 35-40 minutes (leaving extra time for planning and checking). Each essay is followed by detailed comments about its strengths and weaknesses. The most common problems to look for are:

- Students frequently fail to answer the actual question set, and present 'one they made earlier' (the *Blue Peter* answer).
- Many weak essays suffer from a lack of evaluation or commentary.
- On the other hand, sometimes students go too far in the other direction and their essays are all evaluation. Description is vital in demonstrating your knowledge and understanding of the selected topic.
- Don't write 'everything you know' in the hope that something will get credit. Excellence is displayed through selectivity and therefore improvements can often be made by *removing* material which is irrelevant to the question set.

For more ideas about how to write good essays you should consult *Exam Success in AEB Psychology* by Paul Humphreys, in this series.

Practice essay 1

Describe and evaluate the possible contributions of genetic/neurological factors to schizophrenia. (25 marks)
[AEB January 1997]

Candidate's answer

Para. 1: 'Schizophrenia' means 'split personality'. It is a major mental illness affecting approximately one per cent of the population. People with schizophrenia are psychotic, as contact with reality is impaired and they lack insight: many schizophrenic patients go on to commit suicide.

Para. 2: Schizophrenic patients have to take long-term medication. These medicines directly affect brain functioning which shows that there must be something wrong with their brains to start with. Evidence for this can also be seen in the typical behaviour and symptoms of people suffering from this bizarre and distressing disorder.

Para. 3: A major debate in psychology and psychiatry is whether mental illnesses have social/psychological causes or physiological causes. For example, Laing said schizophrenia was a sane response to an insane environment, and although his case studies have supported these theories, there is a lack of evidence from experimental studies. Many of the psychological ideas are difficult to test, but very interesting.

Para. 4: On the other hand, there is evidence that people with schizophrenia have abnormal brains. Brain scan studies indicate that the spaces within the brain (ventricles) are larger in schizophrenia and the brain is correspondingly smaller. These differences are very marked, and are a clear indication of brain damage. Some researchers have suggested that the brain damage must occur very early in life, because it is so extensive, yet it is a puzzle why the illness does not start until early adulthood.

Para. 5: Some researchers have linked the symptoms of schizophrenia to the chemical messengers by which the brain communicates with the body. There is strong evidence that schizophrenia may be related to a malfunction in one of these systems which uses dopamine. The evidence for this is that all of the antipsychotic drugs stimulate dopamine receptors and that drugs that increase dopamine levels, such as amphetamines, can worsen or bring out schizophrenic illnesses. The dopamine theory of schizophrenia is an oversimplification of brain function and has recently been replaced by the serotonin theory. It is not clear whether brain damage and neurotransmitter abnormalities are linked, but I would imagine this is quite likely.

Para. 6: Schizophrenia can definitely be inherited. The evidence for this comes from various studies looking at blood-relatives, twins and adoption. The risk of schizophrenia is bigger if you have a close relative who already has it. Slater and Cowie showed that children of sufferers have a much higher chance of getting schizophrenia, which shows the effect of genetic factors.

Para. 7: Researchers have also have carried out studies of twins, providing proof of genetic causes. Twins are useful because they have a higher incidence of schizophrenia, which is even more pronounced in identical than fraternal twins. However, because twins are so rare, researchers have also looked into adoption. In one study by Wender, children who were adopted by schizophrenics were much more likely to develop schizophrenia themselves, than were children who remained with their natural parents. Also, children of schizophrenics who were adopted by non-schizophrenics had an increased risk of illness in adulthood. Very recently, a gene has been discovered which causes people to develop schizophrenia, and it has also been suggested that there may be two forms of illness, one genetic and the other psychological. Certain viruses may also cause schizophrenia.

Para. 8: Some researchers have looked at the brains of people with schizophrenia using PET scanners. These show that the brain is working abnormally in schizophrenia, and this continues even when symptoms are reduced.

Para. 9: So overall, the evidence from genetic research and neurological research indicates clearly the roles of these factors in causing some people to get schizophrenia.

Examiner's comments

This essay question asks for both description and evaluation. The candidate has done both, though perhaps overlooked the description in a rush to offer evaluation in terms of empirical evidence. The descriptions of each possible contribution lack detail and are very perfunctory. The evaluative points are marred by misunderstanding and error. I would give this essay around 12 out of 25 (5 for description, 7 for evaluation) – likely to be a low grade C.

This information is partly relevant though introduced out of the blue. The fact that medicines work may suggest a physiological cause but is not proof.

Better planning would also produce a more *coherent* answer; the essay begins with material which is, essentially, not relevant to the question. (The opening paragraphs also contain several errors.) This is self-defeating, given the time constraints of an examination, and a sign of poor organisation. In a well-planned essay, there is no room for irrelevancy and the temptation to indulge in this can often be resisted if the essay is planned in outline before writing is begun. The answer really starts at Para.4.

Although there are many ways of answering this question, an effective approach would have been to take a lead from the title: first, describe the genetic research, then evaluate it; second, describe the neurological work, then evaluate that; finally, round off the essay with an overall evaluation, which may include a comment to the effect that genetic and neurological approaches are not mutually exclusive. Alternatively you may want to point out that a stress-diathesis model of the cause of schizophrenia combines the genetic/neurological evidence with psychosocial theories and this may be the best approach to understanding the nature of the illness.

We now consider the answer paragraph by paragraph for specific points:

Para. 1: Schizophrenia does not mean split personality. The majority of people with schizophrenia do not commit suicide.

Para. 2: This material is irrelevant to the question. The fact that drugs may be effective does not mean that the underlying problem is necessarily physiological (although this is likely).

Para. 3: Again, the material is largely irrelevant to this question. The last comment could apply to many other approaches to schizophrenia.

Para. 4: A potentially useful paragraph which includes several misunderstandings: the differences in brain structure are actually very small, and are found in only a proportion of individuals. The last point is a good one, but should have been developed.

Para. 5: The writer needs to be more clear about how this work can be related to the neurological research, otherwise it could be argued that the neurotransmitter research is about function rather than structure. The last sentence suggests that the writer has not understood this subtle but important point.

Para. 6: Schizophrenia is not inherited, although the predisposition to develop it may be. Some data or statistics would aid this paragraph.

Para. 7: Twins do not have a higher incidence of schizophrenia. The important measure is the concordance rate. The way that Wender's study is reported would suggest that schizophrenia can be acquired from adoptive parents, which is the opposite of what his group actually reported. The search for single genes has thus far been unsuccessful. Viral theories have also not been supported by research, but evaluation of these ideas is absent.

Para. 8: A valid comment but totally of out place. This should have been mentioned after Para. 4.

Para. 9: This is not an appropriate concluding paragraph, neither is it factually accurate. The chance to tie things together has been lost. A useful tip is to try to ensure that you conclude your essay by specifically answering the question, in summary form. This gives the impression of a thorough answer even if earlier sections of your essay are below par.

Practice essay 2

Describe and evaluate possible contributions of social/psychological factors to *either* any one eating disorder *or* any one anxiety disorder. (24 marks)

[AEB 1998]

Candidate's answer

Para. 1: For this essay, I am going to talk about phobias. These happen when someone becomes very anxious about a particular thing or place. A good example is agoraphobia, which is fear of open spaces. This phobia often causes panic attacks. The person hates being outside, and may have a panic attack if they are unable to get back indoors. Like most other types of anxiety disorder, the person feels sweaty and their heart beats very quickly. In fact, they may show many features of nervous system arousal. In the worst cases, the person may actually pass out.

Para. 2: So much for describing phobias. What about the causes? There would seem to be several: Freud proposed that phobias result from unconscious inner conflicts, which stem from wanting to do something you know you shouldn't. 'Little Hans' was a good example because he would not leave his house (agoraphobia), because he secretly wanted to have sex with his mother, but he knew his Dad wouldn't approve.

Para. 3: Watson and Rayner said that phobias were caused by faulty learning. They based their theory on Pavlov, who conditioned dogs to salivate to the sound of a bell. Well, Watson and Rayner did the same thing to a boy called Albert, only they made him frightened of a rabbit by making a loud noise every time he stroked it. Unfortunately it has not proved easy to repeat this demonstration with other boys so this seems an unlikely cause of all phobias in general.

Para. 4: Mowrer has a two stage theory. He says that conditioning (as above) gives people the phobia in the first place, but they keep it because the process of avoiding the phobic stimulus is rewarding in itself. For example, with agoraphobia, after the initial panic attack, the person avoids the open space, and the absence of panic is itself rewarding. The combination of classical and operant conditioning makes a lot of sense.

Para. 5: According to Seligman, phobias are just excessive responses to things which our ancient ancestors would have found frightening, such as wild animals or sharp things. He says that humans are innately ready to develop certain phobias if the situation arises. This theory seems plausible to me, but does not say why some people do get a phobia and others don't.

Para. 6: Yet another psychological approach is cognitive. Beck says people become phobic because they think negatively, always seeing potential harm in things, which other people don't mind. It may be that just thinking about anxiety makes people more anxious. For example, if you are worried, and you feel your heart beating, this may make you think you are about to have a heart attack, which will make you more nervous, and so on.

Para. 7: A final approach is to look at brain chemistry. Here, the idea is that too much or too little of certain chemicals leads to anxiety. A good example is noradrenaline, which, if given to normal people makes them have panic attacks. This fits in with the fact that antidepressants can also cause panic attacks, which as I mentioned earlier, are related to phobias. Recently it has been suggested that serotonin is also implicated, because it is known to control the body's response to stress.

Para. 8: As you can see, there are lots of different theories about phobias. Fortunately, phobias are rare, and easy to treat, so do not really present a serious problem unlike depression.

Comments

On first reading, you may think this essay is quite good. The question asks for description and evaluation, and we get a little of each. The answer contains a lot of information, and most of the main ideas are mentioned. It might receive a mark of about 13 out of 25, earning 6 for the descriptive element and 7 for the evaluative element. Both description and evaluation are right on the boundary of bottom/top band 2. The element of breadth just about compensates for the lack of depth/detail. Probably a grade C response.

On the other hand, the material is not always factually accurate (antidepressants do not cause panic attacks). The answer is also written in a slightly chatty style, with items of personal opinion substituting for research evidence (as in the concluding comments in Para. 4 and Para. 5). The examiner will want to reward the student for their breadth of knowledge, but will feel uneasy about awarding a high mark in view of the lack of detail in both the descriptive and evaluative elements of this answer.

The essay could easily have been improved by making the middle section less like a list; by ensuring that the strengths and weaknesses of each approach were spelt out; and by finishing the essay with an evaluative summary which shows the examiner that the candidate has thought about the relative merits of each of the approaches and is 'on top' of the material.

We now consider the essay paragraph by paragraph for specific points:

Para. 1: Quite a good opening, although the question does not actually require much description of the disorder. This sets the scene, and suggests that the writer knows about the main features of anxiety disorders.

Para. 2: There are several theories, rather than several causes. Freud's theory lacks clarity and is not evaluated.

Para. 3: This paragraph lacks detail and seems rushed. Does the candidate really understand how classical conditioning might lead to phobias?

Para. 4: As with the previous paragraph this one lacks both detail and any proper evaluation.

Para. 5: If this suggests some sort of evolutionary or genetic influence, this would have been a good time to introduce the whole issue of whether some people have a genetic vulnerability to develop anxiety disorders.

Para. 6: No evaluation.

Para. 7: A good stab at this material, but one key error is that antidepressants do not cause panic attacks; in fact they are often used as a treatment for panic disorder.

Para. 8: This was the last chance for the candidate to redeem the situation by providing a comprehensive summary and evaluation of the theories presented. This opportunity was wasted and, instead, we are misinformed that phobias are rare (whereas they are quite common) and easy to treat. Phobias can be treated effectively, but so too can depressive illnesses.

l points

plan your answer
organise the material in a natural progression
write a thoughtful summary tying up all the loose ends
make sure you have answered the question

t go off at a tangent
substitute personal opinion for research evidence
include irrelevant material
spend too long on any one answer

GOOD LUCK IN YOUR EXAMINATIONS!

Glossary

The first occurrence of each of these terms is highlighted in **bold** type in the main text.

acute episode A period when an individual's symptoms are particularly prominent. A flare-up of symptoms.

aetiology The study of the causes of disease.

amphetamine psychosis A short-lasting schizophrenia-like illness brought about by excess use of amphetamine ('speed').

anhedonia The inability to derive pleasure.

antipsychotic medication Drugs to treat psychotic conditions such as schizophrenia. All these drugs interfere with brain dopamine systems.

atypical neuroleptics The term used to describe a group of newer drugs used to treat schizophrenia, which generally have fewer side-effects than the earlier neuroleptics.

autonomic nervous system (ANS) That part of the nervous system which is not directly under conscious control, instead controlling (for example) heart rate or dilation of the pupil.

Bedlam A slang term that signifies chaos or mayhem. A contraction of 'Bethlehem Royal Infirmary', an institution set up in the Middle Ages to house the mentally ill.

biofeedback A psychological procedure in which an individual receives overt information about some usually concealed physiological process, such as heart rate or blood pressure.

biological symptoms A term used to identify somatic, or bodily, features of mental illness, such as weight loss or sleep disturbance.

case study The qualitative approach in which a small number of individuals are researched in detail, often by interview and behavioural observation.

catharsis The process of getting clients to discuss concerns whilst under hypnosis in an effort to unburden them of damaging subconscious conflict.

chromosomes Comprising DNA and protein, these carry many hundred individual genes. Humans inherit twenty-three from each parent, and therefore normally have forty-six chromosomes.

classical (Pavlovian) conditioning The form of learning illustrated by Pavlov, who taught a dog to salivate to the sound of a bell by repeatedly pairing the presentation of food with the bell.

clinical psychology A profession for which the usual qualifications are an honours degree in psychology and a master's degree in clinical psychology. Clinical psychologists may work either in hospitals or the community.

cognitive (behavioural) therapy A psychological therapy based on the ideas of Beck, aimed at changing patterns of thinking in individuals. The addition of practical or homework exercises makes cognitive therapy 'behavioural'.

community care The principle of attempting, whenever possible, to provide mental health services outside the hospital setting and close to the patient's home.

concordance A measure of the extent to which twins are similar in respect of some behavioural or physical trait.

dementia praecox Kraepelin's term for what we would now call schizophrenia.

dichotic listening task The type of task in which (usually distinct or different) auditory stimuli are presented simultaneously to each ear.

diurnal mood variation   A pattern of mood fluctuation related to the time of day.

dysthymia   A less severe but more long-lasting form of depression.

dizygotic twins   Another term for fraternal (non-identical) twins, no more genetically alike than brothers and sisters.

eclecticism   The practice of borrowing procedures or treatments from different paradigms, if they seem to work.

electro-convulsive therapy (ECT)   The process of artificially inducing an epileptic seizure by the application of electric current to the head. An effective and rapid treatment for severe depression.

endocrine   Hormonal. An endocrine gland secretes hormones.

factor analysis   A statistical procedure used to understand the ways in which separate symptoms tend to occur in association with one another.

Freudian   A practitioner who adheres to the tenets of the psycho-analytic paradigm.

genes   The individual genetic instructions (rather like recipes) found on chromosomes. Humans have at least 100,000 genes.

hard-wired   In neuroscience, the idea that a particular component of the nervous system has some fixed and unchangeable configuration and function.

idiopathic approach   The approach of clinicians who do not like classification in mental illness.

insulin coma therapy   An early and now discredited treatment for mental illness, in which the individual was put into a coma lasting several days or weeks. The coma was induced by injecting insulin to lower blood-sugar levels.

kappa   A statistic (rather like a correlation coefficient) used to measure reliability.

lanugo   A form of downy hair that develops in patients with severe anorexia nervosa.

manic-depressive psychosis   An illness in which manic and depressive episodes occur; also known as bipolar disorder.

Mendelian   The pattern of inheritance first described by Mendel and linked to dominant and recessive traits.

Mental Health Act   The UK laws governing the compulsory treatment of people with severe mental illnesses, last revised in 1983.

monozygotic twins   Another term for identical twins, having identical genetic constitutions.

moral treatment   The term given to Pinel's treatment, in which patients were treated with respect and efforts were made to appeal to the remnants of their reason.

multi-axial format   As found in DSM, the various axes force the clinician to generate a more complete picture of the social, behavioural and occupational impact of a particular mental condition.

negative schema   A 'mind-set' usually acquired in childhood, which Beck has suggested predisposes an individual to depression (see Beck 1987).

negative symptoms   Symptoms of schizophrenia, such as lack of drive or emotional flattening, marked by an absence or loss of normal function.

negative triad   The pattern of thinking about the self, the world and the future that is typical of a depressed individual.

neurotransmitter system   An identifiable set of brain cells which communicate with each other using a particular neurotransmitter.

neurotransmitters   Chemicals in the nervous system that serve as the means of communication between cells. The mammalian nervous system is estimated to have several hundred different neurotransmitters.

nomothetic approach   The approach of clinicians who use some form of classification system to structure their work.

operant conditioning   The form of learning described by Watson, and later Skinner, in which responses that are positively rewarded are more likely to be repeated.

operational diagnostic criteria   Sets of rules to be used by a clinician in deciding whether or not someone has a particular mental disorder.

phototherapy   A treatment for SAD in which individuals sit in front of a very bright artificial light-source for about two hours each morning.

PKU   Phenylketonuria is a genetically determined metabolic disorder (inherited as a recessive condition) that, if untreated, will result in pronounced mental retardation. In the United Kingdom approximately 1 person in 100 is a carrier for PKU, but only 1 child in 40,000 actually inherits the disorder. It is treated by placing the child on a special diet.

plastic   In neuroscience, a term used to signify the ability of the nervous system to change in some way.

positive symptoms   Symptoms of schizophrenia, such as hallucinations or thought broadcasting, which appear to be in addition to, or imposed on, normal behaviour.

projection   A hypothetical defence mechanism, proposed by Freud, in which an individual's unconscious wishes, desires or emotions are displaced on to someone else.

Psichiatrica Democratica   The political movement founded by the Italian psychiatrist Bassaglia, with the purpose of reforming Italian mental health provision.

psychiatry   The branch of medicine specialising in treatment of people with mental illnesses.

psychogenic   The idea that mental illnesses have psychological (non-physical) origins.

psychotic disorder   A term for mental disorders in which there is discernible loss of contact with reality. Schizophrenia would be one example.

regression   The Freudian concept of returning to an earlier and less-developed level of functioning.

retrovirus   An infectious agent that enters the host's cells and integrates itself into the DNA. The HIV virus is one example.

schizo-affective disorder   The name given to an illness in which symptoms meet the diagnostic criteria for both schizophrenia and depression.

scientist-practitioner   A term used to identify a therapist who operates according to broadly scientific principles.

seasonal affective disorder (SAD)   A form of mood disturbance linked to the amount of daylight. Most marked during winter months.

signs   Considered in conjunction with *symptoms*, signs are features of a condition which are apparent to the clinician but not necessarily of concern to the patient (e.g. slowness of movement or weight loss in depression).

somatogenesis   The principle, first described by Hippocrates, that mental disturbance results from physical disturbances in the brain.

symptoms   Considered in conjunction with *signs*, these are the features of a condition about which the patient is concerned or complains (e.g. hearing voices).

syndromal disorder   A disorder comprising a cluster of symptoms which are often seen together. Schizophrenia is an example.

syndrome The technical term to describe any group of signs and symptoms that are known to be found together.

unconscious mind That aspect of mental function identified by Freud as distinct from the conscious mind, but still capable of influencing behaviour and thought.

Bibliography

Abramson, L.Y., Seligman, M.E. and Teasdale, J.D. (1978) 'Learned helplessness in humans: Critique and reformulation', *Journal of Abnormal Psychology* 87: 49–74.

Agras, W.S., Rossiter, E.M., Arnow, B. *et al.* (1992) 'Pharmacological and cognitive behavioural treatment for bulimia nervosa: A controlled trial', *Americal Journal of Psychiatry* 149: 82–7.

Allebeck, P. (1989) 'Schizophrenia: A life shortening disease', *Schizophrenia Bulletin* 15: 81–9.

Alloy, L.B., Kelly, K.A., Mineka, S. *et al.* (1990) 'Comorbidity in anxiety and depressive disorders: A helplessness/hopelessness perspective', in J.D. Maser and C.R. Cloninger (eds) *Comorbidity in Anxiety and Mood Disorders*, Washington, D.C.: American Psychiatric Press.

Angst, J. (1978) 'The course of affective disorders', in H.M. Van Praag, O.J. Rafealsen, M. Lader and E.K.Sachar (eds) *Handbook of Biological Psychiatry*, NewYork: Dekker.

Barr, C.E., Mednick, S.A. and Munk-Jorgensen, P. (1990) 'Exposure to influenza epidemics during gestation and adult schizophrenia: A forty-year study', *Archives of General Psychiatry* 47: 869–74.

Bateson, G., Jackson, D.D., Haley, J. *et al.* (1956) 'Toward a theory of schizophrenia', *Behavioural Science* 1: 251–64.

Beaumont, P.J.V., Abram, S.F. and Simpson, J.G. (1981) 'The psychosexual histories of adolescent girls and young women with anorexia nervosa', *Psychological Medicine* 11: 131–40.

Bebbington, P., Wilkins, S., Jones, P. *et al.* (1993) 'Life events and psychosis: Initial results from the Camberwell Collaborative Psychosis study', *British Journal of Psychiatry* 162: 72–9.

Beck, A.T. (1987) 'Cognitive models of depression', *Journal of Cognitive Psychotherapy: An International Quarterly* 1: 5–37.

Beck., A.T. and Emery, G. (1985) *Anxiety Disorders and Phobias: A Cognitive Perspective*, New York: Basic Books.

Bemis, K.M. (1978) 'Current approaches to the aetiology and management of anorexia nervosa', *Psychological Bulletin* 85: 593–617.

Bentall, R.P. (1990) 'The illusion of reality: A review and integration of psychological research on hallucinations', *Psychological Bulletin* 107 (1): 82–95.

Bremner, J.D., Innis, R.B., Chin, K. *et al.* (1997) 'Positron emission tomography measurement of cerebral metabolic correlates of yohimbine administration in combat-related post traumatic stress disorder', *Archives of General Psychiatry* 54: 246–54.

Brown, G.W. and Harris, T.O. (1978) *Social Origins of Depression*, London: Tavistock.

Bruch, H. (1974) *Eating Disorders: Anorexia Nervosa and the Person Within*, London: Routledge and Kegan Paul.

Burgess, I.S. (1981) 'The degree of control exerted by phobic and non-phobic verbal stimuli over the recognition behaviour of phobic and non-phobic subjects', *Behaviour Research and Therapy* 19: 233–43.

Chambless, D.L. and Gillis, M.M. (1993) 'Cognitive therapy of anxiety disorders', *Journal of Consulting and Clinical Psychology* 61: 248–60.

Clare, A. (1980) *Psychiatry in Dissent*, 2nd edn, London: Tavistock.

Clark, D.M. (1986) 'A cognitive approach to panic', *Behaviour Research and Therapy* 24: 461–70.

Crisp, A.H. (1977) 'Diagnosis and outcome of anorexia nervosa: The St George's view', *Proceedings of the Royal Society of Medicine* 70: 464–70.

Crow, T.J. (1980) 'Molecular pathology of schizophrenia: More than one disease process?', *British Medical Journal* 12 January: 66–8.

—— (1983) 'Is schizophrenia an infectious disease?' *Lancet* i: 173–5.

—— (1997) 'Is schizophrenia the price that *Homo sapiens* pays for language?', *Schizophrenia Research* 28: 127–41.

Crow, T.J., Done, D.J. and Johnstone, E.C. (1991) 'Schizophrenia and influenza', *Lancet* 338: 116–17.

Crow, T.J., MacMillan, J.F., Johnson, A.L. *et al.* (1986) 'The Northwick Park study of first-episode schizophrenia II. A randomised controlled treatment of prophylactic neuroleptic medication', *British Journal of Psychiatry* 148: 120–7.

Curson, D.A., Barnes, T.R., Bamber, R.W. *et al.* (1985) 'A seven-year follow-up study of MRC "Modecate" trial', *British Journal of Psychiatry* 146: 464–80.

Cutting, J. (1985) 'Systematic review of psychological theories of schizophrenia', in *The Psychology of Schizophrenia*, Edinburgh: Churchill Livingstone, pp. 349–77.

Davison, G.C. (1968) 'Systematic desensitization as a counter-conditioning process', *Journal of Abnormal Psychology*, 73: 91–9.

Deakin, J.F.W. and Graeff, F.G. (1991) '5-HT and mechanisms of defence', *Journal of Psychopharmacology* 5 (4): 305–15.

Depue, R.A. and Monroe, S.M. (1978) 'Learned helplessness in the perspective of the depressive disorders: Conceptual and definitional issues', *Journal of Abnormal Psychology* 87: 3–20.

Done, D.J., Johnstone, E.C., Frith, C.D. *et al.* (1991) 'Complications of pregnancy and delivery in relation to psychosis in adult life: Data from the British perinatal mortality survey sample', *British Medical Journal* 302: 1,576–80.

Egeland, J.A. (1987) 'Bipolar affective disorders linked to DNA markers on chromosome 11', *Nature* 325: 1,004–31.

Elkin, I., Parloff, M.B., Hadley, S.W. *et al.* (1985) 'NIMH treatment of depression collaborative research program', *Archives of General Psychiatry* 42: 305–16.

Eysenck, H.J. (1976) 'The learning theory model of neurosis: A new approach', *Behaviour Research and Therapy* 14: 251–67.

Fairburn, C.G., Jones, R., Peveler, R.C. *et al.* (1991) 'Three psychological treatments for bulimia nervosa: A comparative trial', *Archives of General Psychiatry* 48: 463–9.

Freud, S. (1896) 'Further remarks on the neuro-psychoses of defence'; republished in J. Strachey (ed.) *The Standard Edition of the Complete Psychological Works of Sigmund Freud*, London: Hogarth Press, 1962, vol. 3, pp. 174–85.

—— (1909) 'Analysis of a phobia in a five-year-old boy'; republished in J. Strachey (ed.) *The Standard Edition of the Complete Psychological Works of Sigmund Freud*, London: Hogarth Press, 1962, vol. 10, pp. 3–26.

—— (1917) 'Mourning and melancholia'; republished in J. Strachey (ed.) *The Standard Edition of the Complete Psychological Works of Sigmund Freud*, London: Hogarth Press, 1962, vol. 14, pp. 243–58.

Frith, C.D. (1992) *The Neuropsychology of Schizophrenia*, Hove: Lawrence Erlbaum.

Fromm-Reichmann, F. (1948) 'Notes on the development of treatment of schizophrenics by psychoanalytic psychotherapy', *Psychiatry* 11: 63–273.

Garner, D.M. and Garfinkel, P.E. (1980) 'Socio-cultural factors in the development of anorexia nervosa', *Psychological Medicine* 10: 647–56.

Goldman, H.H. (1992) *Review of General Psychiatry*, 3rd edn, London: Prentice Hall.

Gottesman, I.I. (1991) *Schizophrenia Genesis: The origins of madness*, New York: Freeman.

Gottesman, I.I. and Shields, J. (1972) *Schizophrenia and Genetics: A Twin Vantage Point*, New York: Academic Press.

Henry, J. (1973) *Pathways to Madness*, New York: Vintage Books.

Heston, L.L. (1966) 'Psychiatric disorders in foster home reared children of schizophrenic mothers', *British Journal of Psychiatry* 122: 819–25.

Hibbert, G.A. (1984) 'Ideational components of anxiety, their origin and content', *British Journal of Psychiatry* 144: 618–24.

Hirsch, S.R. (1979) 'Do parents cause schizophrenia?', *Trends in Neuroscience (TINS)* February: 49–52.

Hirsch, S.R. and Leff, J.P. (1975) *Abnormalities in Parents of Schizophrenics*, Institute of Psychiatry Maudsley Monographs No. 22, London: Oxford University Press.

Hodel, B. and Brenner, H.D. (1994) 'Cognitive therapy with schizophrenic patients: Conceptual basis, present state, future directions', *Acta Psychiatrica Scandinavica* 90 (supp. 384): 108–15.

Hodgkinson, S. (1987) 'Molecular genetic evidence for heterogeneity in manic depression', *Nature* 325: 805–6.

Hogarty, G.E., Anderson, C.M., Reiss, D.J. *et al.* (1986) 'Family psychoeducation, social skills training and maintenance chemotherapy in the aftercare treatment of schizophrenia 1: One year effects of a controlled study on relapse and expressed emotion', *Archives of General Psychiatry* 43: 633–42.

—— (1991) 'Family psychoeductaion, social skills training and maintenance chemotherapy in the aftercare treatment of schizophrenia 2: Two year effects of a controlled study on relapse and adjustment', *Archives of General Psychiatry* 48: 340–7.

Hogarty, G.E., Sander, M.S., Kornblith, J. *et al.* (1997) 'Three year trials of personal therapy among schizophrenic patients living with or independent of family: Description of study and effects on relapse of patients', *American Journal of Psychiatry* 154: 1,504–13.

Holland, A.J., Hall, A., Murray, R. *et al.* (1984) 'Anorexia nervosa: A study of thirty-four twin pairs and a set of triplets', *British Journal of Psychiatry* 145: 414–19.

Hsu, L.K. (1990) *Eating Disorders*, New York: Guilford.

Ingleby, D. (ed.) (1981) *Critical Psychiatry*, Harmondsworth: Penguin.

Johns, L.C. (1998) 'Occurrence of hallucinations in a community sample', *Schizophrenia Research* 29 (1–2): 23.

Jones, K. and Poletti, A. (1986) 'Understanding the Italian Experience', *British Journal of Psychiatry* 146: 341–7.

Jones, P., Rodgers, B. and Murray, R. (1994) 'Childhood development risk factors for adult schizophrenia in the British 1946 birth cohort', *Lancet* 344: 1,398–402.

Jung, C.G. (1939) 'On the psychogenesis of schizophrenia', *Journal of Mental Science* 85: 999–1,011.

Kendler, K.S., McGuire, M., Gruenberg, A.M. *et al.* (1994) 'Clinical heterogeneity in schizophrenia and the pattern of psychopathology in relatives: Results from an epidemiologically based family study', *Acta Psychiatrica Scandinavica* 89: 294–300.

Kennedy, J.L., Guiffra, L.A., Moises, H.W. *et al.* (1988) 'Evidence against linkage of schizophrenia to markers on chromosome 5 in a Northern Swedish pedigree', *Nature* 336: 167–9.

Kerwin, R. and Taylor, D. (1996) 'New antipsychotics: A review of their current status and clinical potential', *CNS Drugs* 6 (1): 71–82.

Klein, M. (1934) *The Psychoanalysis of Children*, London: Hogarth.

Kuhn, T.S. (1962) *The Structure of Scientific Revolutions*, Chicago, IL: University of Chicago Press.

Kuipers, E., Fowler, D., Garety, P. *et al.* (1998) 'London–East Anglia randomised controlled trial of cognitive-behavioural therapy for psychosis: (iii) Follow-up and economic evaluation at eighteen months', *British Journal of Psychiatry* 173: 61–8.

Laing, R.D. (1971) *The Politics of the Family*, London: Tavistock.

Laing, R.D. and Esterson, A. (1970) *Sanity, Madness and the Family*, 2nd edn, London: Pelican.

Lewinsohn, P.M., Roberts, R.E., Seeley, J.R. *et al.* (1994) 'Adolescent psychopathology: (2) Psychosocial risk factors for depression', *Journal of Abnormal Psychology* 103: 302–15.

Lewis, S.W. and Murray, R.M. (1987) 'Obstetric complications, neurodevelopmental deviance and risk of schizophrenia', *Journal of Psychiatric Research* 21: 413–21.

Liddle, P.F. (1987) 'The symptoms of chronic schizophrenia: A re-examination of the positive–negative dichotomy', *British Journal of Psychiatry* 151: 145–51.

Lidz, T., Cornelison, A., Terry, D. *et al.* (1958) 'Intrafamilial environment of the schizophrenic patient: (vi) The transmission of irrationality', *Archives of Neurology and Psychiatry* 79: 305–16.

Liem, J. (1974) 'Effects of verbal communications of parents and children: A comparison of normal and schizophrenic families', *Journal of Consulting and Clinical Psychology* 42: 438–50.

McCreadie, R.G., Hall, D.J., Berry, I.J. *et al.* (1992) 'The Nithsdale schizophrenia surveys: (x) Obstetric complications, family history and abnormal movements', *British Journal of Psychiatry* 161: 799–805.

McGuffin, P. and Katz, R. (1986) 'Nature, nurture and affective disorder', in J.F.W. Deakin (ed.) *The Biology of Depression*, London: Gaskell, pp. 26–52.

McGuire, P.K., Shah, G.M. and Murray, R.M. (1993) 'Increased blood flow in Broca's area during auditory hallucinations in schizophrenia', *Lancet* 342: 703–6.

Meehl, P.E. (1962) 'Schizotaxia, schizotypy, schizophrenia', *American Psychologist* 17: 827–38.

Mendelwicz, J. and Rainer, J.D. (1977) 'Adoption study supporting genetic transmission of manic depressive illness', *Nature* 268: 327–9.

Metalsky, G.I., Haberstadt, L.J. and Abramson, L.Y. (1987) 'Vulnerability and invulnerability to depressive mood reactions: Toward a more powerful test of the diathesis-stress and causal mediation components of the reformulation theory of depression', *Journal of Personality and Social Psychology* 52: 386–93.

Metalsky, G.I., Joiner, T.E., Hardin, T.S. *et al.* (1993) 'Depressive reactions to failure in a naturalistic setting: A test of the hopelessness and self esteem theories of depression', *Journal of Abnormal Psychology* 102: 101–9.

Mikhliner, M. and Solomon, Z. (1988) 'Attributional style and PTSD', *Journal of Abnormal Psychology* 97: 308–13.

Minuchin, S., Rosman, B. and Baker, L. (1978) *Psychosomatic families: Anorexia nervosa in context*, Cambridge, MA: Harvard University Press.

Mowrer, O.H. (1939) 'A stimulus-response analysis of anxiety and its role as a reinforcing agent', *Psychological Review* 46: 553–65.

Muijen, M. (1996) 'Care of schizophrenia in the community', paper given at British Association for Pharmacology, Leicester, April.

Murphy, D.G., Daly, E.M., Van Amelsvoort, T. *et al.* (1998) 'Functional neuroanatomical dissociation of verbal, visual and spatial working memory', *Schizophrenia Research* 29 (1–2): 105.

Murray, R.M., Lewis, S.W., Owen, M.J. *et al.* (1988) 'The neurodevelopmental origins of dementia praecox', in P. Bebbington and P. McGuffin (eds) *Schizophrenia: The Major Issues*, Oxford: Heinemann/Mental Health Foundation, pp. 90–106.

Okubo, Y., Suhara, T., Suzuki, K. *et al.* (1997) 'Decreased prefrontal dopamine D1 receptors in schizophrenia revealed by PET', *Nature* 385: 634.

Paykel, E.S. and Hollyman, J.A. (1984) 'Life events and depression: A psychiatric view', *Trends in Neurosciences* December: 478–81.

Peters, E., Day, S., Linney, Y. *et al.* (1998) 'The correlates of delusional thinking: Preliminary findings using the PDI in the normal population', *Schizophrenia Research* 29 (1, 2): 39–40.

Price, J. (1968) 'The genetics of depressive behaviour', in A. Coppen and S. Walk (eds) *Recent Developments in the Affective Disorders*, Special Publication No. 2, *British Journal of Psychiatry*.

Raz, S. and Raz, N. (1990) 'Structural brain abnormalities in the major psychoses: A quantitative review of the evidence from computerised imaging', *Psychological Bulletin* 108: 93–108.

Reynolds, G.P. (1989) 'Beyond the dopamine hypothesis', *British Journal of Psychiatry* 155: 305–16.

Rohme, M.A. and Escher, A.D. (1989) 'Hearing voices', *Schizophrenia Bulletin* 15 (2): 209–16.

Rosenthal, D. (1971) 'Two adoption studies of heredity in the schizophrenic disorders', in M. Bleuler and J. Angst (eds) *The Origins of Schizophrenia*, Bern: Huber, pp. 21–34.

Sachar, E.J. and Baron, M. (1978) 'The biology of affective disorders', *Annual Review of Neuroscience* 2: 505–18.

Sanderson, W.C., Rapee, R.M. and Barlow, D.H. (1989) 'The influence of an illusion of control on panic attacks induced by inhalation of 5.5% CO_2 enriched air', *Archives of General Psychiatry* 46: 157–62.

Sartorius, N., Kaelber, C.T., Cooper, J.E. *et al.* (1993) 'Progress towards achieving a common language in psychiatry: Results from the field trial of the clinical guidelines accompanying the WHO classification of mental and behavioural disorders in ICD-10', *Archives of General Psychiatry* 50: 115–24.

Sartorius, N., Shapiro, R. and Jablonsky, A. (1974) 'The international pilot study of schizophrenia', *Schizophrenia Bulletin* 2: 21–35.

Seeman, P. (1980) 'Dopamine receptors and the dopamine hypothesis of schizophrenia', *Pharmacological Reviews* 32: 229–313.

Seligman, M.E. (1971) 'Phobias and preparedness', *Behaviour Therapy* 2: 307–20.

—— (1974) 'Depression and learned helplessness', in R.J. Friedman and M.M. Katz (eds) *The Psychology of Depression: Contemporary Theory and Research*, Washington, D.C.: Winston-Wiley.

Shepherd, M., Watt, D. and Falloon, I. (1989) 'The natural history of schizophrenia: A five year follow-up study of outcome and prediction in a representative sample of schizophrenics', *Psychological Medicine Monograph Supplement* 15: 1–46

Sherrington, R., Brynjolffson, J., Peterson, H. *et al.* (1988) 'Localisation of a susceptibility locus for schizophrenia on chromosome 5', *Nature* 336: 164–7.

Slater, E. and Cowie, V. (1971) *The Genetics of Mental Disorder*, Oxford: Oxford University Press.

Slater, E. and Shields, J. (1969) 'Genetic aspects of anxiety', in *Studies of Anxiety*, Special Publication No. 3, *British Journal of Psychiatry*.

Snyder, S.H. (1976) 'The dopamine hypothesis of schizophrenia: Focus on the dopamine receptor', *American Journal of Psychiatry* 133 (2): 197–202.

Solomon, Z., Mikulincev, M. and Flum, H. (1988) 'Negative life events, coping response and combat-related psychopathology: A prospective study', *Journal of Abnormal Psychology* 97: 302–7.

Spence, S.A., Brooks, D.J., Hirsch, S.R. *et al.* (1997) 'A PET study of voluntary movement in schizophrenic patients experiencing passivity phenomena (delusions of alien control)', *Brain* 120: 1,997–2,011.

Stirling, J.D. (1994) 'Schizophrenia and expressed emotion', *Perspective in Psychiatric Care* 30 (2): 20–5.

Stirling, J.D., Hellewell, J.S. and Hewitt J. (1997) 'Verbal memory impairment in schizophrenia: No sparing of short-term recall', *Schizophrenia Research* 25: 85–95.

Stirling, J.D., Hellewell, J.S. and Quraishi, N. (1998) 'Self-monitoring dysfunction and the schizophrenic symptoms of alien control', *Psychological Medicine* 28: 675–83.

Stirling, J.D., Tantam, D., Thomas, P. *et al.* (1993) 'Expressed emotion and schizophrenia: The ontogeny of EE during an eighteen month follow-up', *Psychological Medicine* 23: 771–8.

Sullivan, H.S. (1924) 'Schizophrenia: Its conservative and malignant features', *American Journal of Psychiatry* 88: 519–40.

Sullivan, P.F., Bulik, C.M. and Kendler, K.S. (1998) 'Genetic epidemiology of bingeing and vomiting', *British Journal of Pychiatry* 173: 75–9.

Szasz, T.S. (1960) 'The myth of mental illness', *American Psychologist* 15: 113–18.

—— (1985) 'Psychiatry: Rhetoric or reality?', *The Lancet* **ii**: 711–12.

Szmukler, G.I. and Russell, G.F. (1986) 'Outcome and prognosis of anorexia nervosa', in K.D. Brownell and J.P. Goreyt (eds) *Handbook of Eating Disorders: Physiology, Psychology and Treatment of Obesity, Anorexia and Bulimia*, New York: Basic Books.

Teasdale, J.D., Fennell, M.J., Hibbert, G.A. *et al.* (1984) 'Cognitive therapy for major depressive disorder in primary care', *British Journal of Psychiatry* 44: 400–6.

Theander, S. (1970) 'Anorexia nervosa: A psychiatric investigation of female patients', *Acta Psychiatrica Scandinavica*, supp. 214.

Thomas, C.S. and Lewis, S. (1998) 'Which atypical antipsychotic?', *British Journal of Psychiatry* 172: 106–9.

Torrey, E.F., Bowler, A.E. and Rawlings, R. (1992) 'Schizophrenia and the 1957 influenza epidemic', *Schizophrenia Research* 6: 100.

Vaughn, C.E. and Leff, J.P. (1976) 'The influence of family and social factors on the course of psychiatric illness', *British Journal of Psychiatry* 129: 125–37.

Walker, E.F., Grimes, K.E., Davis, D.M. *et al.* (1993) 'Childhood precursors of schizophrenia: Facial expressions of emotion', *American Journal of Psychiatry* 150: 1,654–60.

Watson, J.B. and Rayner, R. (1920) 'Conditioned emotional reactions', *Journal of Experimental Psychology* 3: 1–14.

Wender, P.H., Rosenthal, D., Kety, S.S. *et al.* (1974) 'Crossfostering: A research strategy for clarifying the role of genetic and experimental factors in the aetiology of schizophrenia', *Archives of General Psychiatry* 31: 121–8.

WHO (World Health Organisation) (1979) *Schizophrenia: An International Follow-up Study*, Geneva: Wiley.

Wong, D.F., Wagner, H.N., Tune, L.E. *et al.* (1986) 'Positron emission tomography reveals elevated D_2 dopamine receptors in drug-naïve schizophrenics', *Science* 234: 1,558–62.

Zervas, I. and Fink, M. (1991) 'Electro-convulsive therapy', *Current Opinion in Psychiatry* 4: 14–19.

Index